LEONARDO DiCAPRIO

Douglas Thompson

BERKLEY BOULEVARD BOOKS, NEW YORK

for Dandy

LEONARDO DICAPRIO

A Berkley Boulevard Book / published by arrangement with
André Deutsch, Ltd.

PRINTING HISTORY
First published in 1998 by Chameleon, André Deutsch Limited, a subsidiary of VCI plc.
Berkley Boulevard trade paperback edition / June 1998

The Penguin Putnam Inc. World Wide Web site address is
http://www.penguinputnam.com

ISBN: 0-425-16752-6

BERKLEY BOULEVARD
Berkley Boulevard Books are published by
The Berkley Publishing Group, a member of Penguin Putnam Inc.,
200 Madison Avenue, New York, New York 10016.
BERKLEY BOULEVARD and its logo are trademarks belonging to
Berkley Publishing Corporation.

PRINTED IN THE UNITED STATES OF AMERICA

10 9 8 7 6 5 4 3 2 1

CONTENTS

PROLOGUE
ALL FOR ONE
"I'M NOT SAYING I'M PERFECT"
LEONARDO DiCAPRIO
1997

PARIS, SUMMER, 1997

The buzz, a catchy movie-speak of pidgin French-English-Italian, almost drowned out the more polite conversations taking place in the intimate bar of the L'Hotel International. Even here in Boulevard Victor-Hugo's most famous showbusiness hotel, heads were turning and nodding.

Gerard Depardieu, a national institution in France, Britain's Jeremy Irons, America's John Malkovich and Ireland's Gabriel Byrne were in the hotel, a United Nations of movie talent.

But it was the younger man, the boy-like figure with the grown-up confidence, who was attracting all the attention. Paris is familiar with celebrity, usually disdainful of Hollywood stars and entourages, but the hotel crowd could not stop themselves watching and talking about the six-foot tall, lanky figure in the black Emporia Armani T-shirt and jeans and blue Nike running shoes.

Depardieu was wielding the wine list at the bar and displaying his self-taught, vintage knowledge about the Cabernets and Sauvignons.

Leonardo DiCaprio sipped a Diet Coke as he frisked the room with his piercing blue eyes.

For the young man born just off Sunset Boulevard in Hollywood, the Boulevard Victor Hugo in the centre of Paris was simply another location. He was unaware that word of his whereabouts was flying around the city from the panoramic rooftop bar of the nearby Hilton to the historic and famous St Germain cafes.

At 22, DiCaprio was already an icon in France.

And for the rest of the movie-going world he is an established superstar, having arrived, it seems, out of nowhere. Leonardo DiCaprio is a punk, the twenty-first century rebel in the retro 1970s T-shirt with the 1950s attitude of James Dean and Brando, and the idol of the world's teenage girls and Hollywood's box office. He is also a gay icon with a world-wide 'pink' following. He has filled the vacuum in Hollywood for an apparently unconventional leading man, a cult hero, who also has a natural appeal to mass mainstream audiences.

DiCaprio is *the* world-wide teenage heart-throb, easily eclipsing music stars like Boyzone and Peter André and sporting heroes such as UK footballer and Spice Girl boyfriend David Beckham. His image is on bedroom walls from Milwaukee to Moscow to Manchester, from Tokyo to Toulouse to Tallahassee.

He is the 'It' boy – and says, not always convincingly, that it has all happened through the happenstance of being in the right movie at the right time, rather than as a result of some heavily plotted career campaign.

In Hollywood, business analysts predict that every movie he appears in will make at least $10 million at the American box-office in its opening weekend – just from the turn-out of his fans. Reaction in Europe and Asia is as hot. Britain's *Empire* movie magazine voted him number

☆ DiCaprio, 1998: Elected by *U.S.* magazine as 'quite simply the world's biggest heart-throb'.

4

15 in the '100 Sexiest Stars in the World' chart published in June, 1997 — and that was before he starred as the doomed lover ('a spectacular James Dean style of a role', according to UK movie analyst David Gibsone) in *Titanic*, the most expensive film ever made.

He was beaten by 'Uncle' Tom Cruise and 'Grandad' Mel Gibson in that 1997 chart but was streets ahead of his closest contemporaries like Johnny Depp and Ewan McGregor, and way ahead of George Clooney and Daniel Day-Lewis. The chart included sexy men *and* women. More than the Brat Pack stars of the 1980s or the younger leading men at the close of the 1990s, he has

☆ **An early smoulder from the star. Award-winning Titanic director James Cameron calls him 'the Gary Cooper of his generation' and says 'I met him and just loved him.'**

built a bridge over Tinseltown demographics and has already established himself as a cultural metaphor. For Hollywood he is the great, bright hope, the New Age star of the millennium, the king of 'Young Hollywood'. It's a business in which Tom Cruise has now reached ageing leading man status, and Keanu Reeves, who, not so long ago, it seemed, was a youth icon, is fast approaching the other side of Hollywood Hills.

DiCaprio is young but around an age when Marlon Brando was becoming a star in *A Streetcar Named Desire*, Robert Mitchum was creating his image as a flawed film noir leading man in *Out of the Past* and John Travolta was winning an Oscar nomination for *Saturday Night Fever*. Hollywood feeds – and sustains itself – on youth and talent.

For the moment DiCaprio has both on his side.

So Paris was buzzing. DiCaprio was in town to make his 'Mel Gibson breakthrough', an allusion to Gibson's Oscar bonanza *Braveheart*. What's more, hot on the heels of the $216-million-dollar-budgeted *Titanic*, his new release the romantic costume adventure *The Man in the Iron Mask* was filmed entirely in France.

Most of the work was completed on eight sound stages at the Studios Arpajon near Paris and on location at the Chateau de Vaux le Victome and Fontainebleau. The film-makers knew all about DiCaprio's audience appeal – in the picture he plays two roles: the mystery title character and the hiss-inducing evil King Louis XIV. Irons, Malkovich and Depardieu play Aramis, Athos and Porthos, the Three Musketeers, with Gabriel Byrne as their Captain, D'Artagnan. Randall Wallace, who scripted *Braveheart*, makes his début as a director, following the classic lines of the story in his own screenplay of the Alexandre Dumas novel. DiCaprio's Louis XIV has succeeded the benevolent Louis XIII whom the Musketeers served. He is arrogant and his attitude threatens the throne of France and, in the tradition of such movies, the future of France itself ... as well as that of the exceptional Anne Parillaud as the Queen Mother, Anne d'Autriche. The plot and action never slow as the Musketeers ride off to rescue a strange prisoner from an Alcatraz-style island prison fortress ...

'After *Titanic*, which was a gigantic special effects exercise and a love story on the scale of *Dr Zhivago*, this was just out and out adventure, brilliant fun,' said DiCaprio during a break in filming at Studios Arpajon. 'It's the sort of movie that you dream of being able to make. Every kid has had imaginary sword fights, been a pirate or a buccaneer. This was my chance to do all of that with real horses and swords, everything you could imagine. It was really cool. And playing two parts – I'm not giving the plot away, they won't let me!', he laughs.

'Let's just say it was altogether very different characters.'

There is no in-built audience for costume dramas when contemporary action-adventure and sci-fi themes remain the winners at the box-office lottery. Nevertheless, DiCaprio immediately signed-up for the film.

He likes to take chances, but not the self-destructive ones with drugs and unsafe sex with which the gossip columns have often branded him. The rock 'n' roll bible *Rolling Stone* magazine said in 1994 that DiCaprio was flirting with a tragic end, asserting, 'he seems poised to assume the mantle of River Phoenix.' But he appears the opposite. Screenwriter James Torback who wrote *Bugsy* for Warren Beatty defends his young friend: 'He's a very cunning, calculating, shrewd and smart guy. He would run away from anybody and anything that might sabotage him. He does not want to fail.'

He also wants to survive.

Despite this, on 19 June 1996, he stood at the open door of a plane flying 12,368 feet above California's Santa Monica Mountains – and jumped.

He was tandem, jumping, sky-diving with an instructor. It was a 'partying' thing to celebrate the twenty-first birthday of his actor friend Justin Herwick.

He was about 5,200 feet above the ground when he pulled his parachute rip cord. The chute didn't open. DiCaprio looked up at the heavens for help. It was there. Instructor Harley Powell who was 'piggy-back' with him postponed opening his parachute and worked on DiCaprio's. They plummeted down for 23 seconds ('that was really scary'). Powell cut off DiCaprio's useless parachute with a Swiss Army knife. As it was whipped away in the wind they continued free-falling. Powell freed DiCaprio's emergency 'chute, yanked his own open, and they both floated down.

Later, DiCaprio said: 'I like to do things that scare me but sky-diving is just the sickest thing. I made a little video afterward where I look into the camera all jittery and go: "Leonardo, if you're watching this, this is your last time sky-diving. It's your first life-and-death experience. I want you to learn from it."'

At the time an agitated Justin Herwick reported: 'I thought I was going to lose my best friend.'

'No way', said a determined Leonardo DiCaprio. 'I'm just beginning to fly ...'

LEOMANIA

"WITH LEO IT'S LIKE THE BEATLES"
HOLLYWOOD PRODUCER MARTIN BROWN

With the millennium fast approaching Leonardo DiCaprio is one of the most sought after actors in the world, the most wanted of his generation. That, in his opinion, was cool. But no big thing.

Born on 11 November 1974 (a Scorpio compatible romance-wise with Cancer and Pisces), he had celebrated his twenty-third birthday just a few weeks before his landmark year of 1998. Looking wide awake and bubbly in a suite at a Beverly Hills hotel he shrugs off all the acclaim. 'I realize my age and the fact that already I've done quite a few films. Some of them are pretty good and you start to get a little proud of yourself. I'm happy where I am right now. I realize that people my age are looking at some of my stuff so it's a cool thing. I just want to keep doing what I'm doing and hopefully people will watch my movies,' he adds.

Nevertheless, he is more aware than his words allow. 'I sometimes think he never was a baby, a kid', says his mother Irmelin. She helps manage his career and is the antithesis of the stage mum. There is nothing obsessive or pushy about the apparently happy blonde although she is fiercely protective of her son.

'My mother came over from Germany during World War Two when she was very young, about eleven (DiCaprio's 'secret' middle name is 'Wilhelm'). She came over to America and started going to college in New York and that's where she and my Dad met. Once they had me, they moved to Los Angeles because they heard it was such a great place. They moved right into the heart of Hollywood because they figured that's where all the great stuff was going on in this town. Meanwhile, it was the most disgusting place to be. When I grew up I lived in the ghettos of Hollywood at places which were the crack cocaine and prostitution crossroads of Los Angeles,' he says reflectively.

Shrugging off the media's attempt to pigeon-hole him, DiCaprio goes on, 'Hollywood Brat? Far from it. That's fantasy. I was an import — like my parents. My Dad's a full Italian and I wanted to visit Capri because that's *di Caprio*, that's my name, my roots.

'I got my first name when they were both on honeymoon in Italy. My mom felt me kicking as they were looking at a Leonardo da Vinci painting at the Uffizi in Florence and took it as a message ...'

Yet it wasn't a classical upbringing for Leonardo DiCaprio although at first his parents thought he would be a painter: their '*psychic rhythm*' told them that he would be an important twenty-first century artist. His parents were mystical, 'psychic rhythm' sort of people in the 1960s, who had been into the flower power movement in America and enjoying a hippie lifestyle. In 1997, George DiCaprio still wore his greying hair to his elbows. He separated from his wife when their son was one year old but they brought him up amicably within

☆ 'You looking at me?' And why not? A straight-between-the-eyes close encounter with Leo.

☆ Dangerous in denim: an early Leo fashion shoot.

their easy-going, and the generally fairly unconventional lifestyles they enjoyed.

They have never divorced. George DiCaprio lives with exercise physiologist Peggy Farrar and Leo's 'stepbrother' Adam in Hollywood, two miles away from where his son stayed with the shy, soft-spoken Irmelin in a ranch-style home in East Hollywood. It has a modest swimming pool and none of the wild trappings associated with young fame and Tinseltown pay-days. But the place he calls 'the hacienda' and his own new apartment in North Hollywood which he moved into in March 1995, are a positive upgrade from the tough East Hollywood areas where he grew up. There, the rows of Spanish-style bungalows are overlooked from Griffith Park (where James Dean and Natalie Wood filmed pivotal scenes of *Rebel Without a Cause*) and the now defunct Griffith Park Zoo. From the outside they seem quaint. Inside the rooms are small, claustrophobic, the windows usually shuttered, the wheezing air-conditioning units losing the cooling game with the inner-city heat.

His parents' bohemian lifestyle was not lavish much: 'We were in the poorhouse,' confesses

☆ The DiCaprio hormonal radar alert.

☆ At work with the Oscar ladies, Meryl Streep and Diane Keaton, in the moving drama *Marvin's Room*.

DiCaprio. 'I would walk to my playground and see a guy open up his trench coat with a thousand syringes. I saw some major homosexual activity from my friend's balcony when I was five and to this day it's an imprint on my mind. I don't do drugs, I've never done drugs – I will always want to make some sort of statement against heroin. It's become a craze among young people and it's wrong.'

On a trip around his old neighbourhood known for its 'syringe alley' environment, graffiti, bullets and gangs, he points out his 'historical sights'. His tour stops at one rundown bungalow: 'That's where I lived from age eleven to fifteen. There's my old basketball net. And that's where I used to get on the roof and throw avocados at people. That "Thrifty" store used to be a "Ralph's" supermarket – I stole my first piece of bubblegum there but I stopped stealing because I believed in karma. I'm curious about Buddhism. My brother is into it and he's constantly preaching to me. I want to get into it but I also want to know a lot more about it. I'd say it was the best religion – there I go!', he laughs. 'Seriously, I'm still looking into it.'

His East Hollywood home tour continues: 'This abandoned lot is where I used to play with car parts and get beat up. Over there is the "House of Billiards", one of the crack cocaine addicts' hang-outs.' He moves on and at the end of an alley is an even more rundown bungalow: 'My first house. Smells like *huevos rancheros* [Mexican-style fried eggs].

'This is where I come from which is why the money they throw around doesn't get me. What would I need all that money for anyway? I'd be miserable in a mansion all by myself. I don't want to sound like I'm some underprivileged kid but you learn certain values.

'Like not accepting that because you're in a hotel you have to pay five dollars for a Diet Coke. Just go down the block for a three-dollar six-pack.

'On the other hand I have a 600-dollar leather jacket and a 35,000-dollar Jeep [a metallic blue Jeep Grand Cherokee with a cellular phone and its own public address system]. Rags to riches, eh?'

DiCaprio, despite all the fuss and his current status as the most popular leading man at the movies – a status he is set to maintain over the next few

Leo is on a quest to see how many things he can do in life and not do them straight.

☆ There's method in her madness... Meryl Streep, as Leo's mixed-up mother in *Marvin's Room*, reveals some home secrets.

years – glides on a comparatively even keel. 'We did all the craziness for him', says his mother. His father, who shared rooms with Lou Reed and the Velvet Underground in New York, produced avant-garde comic books and was a friend of writers like the legendary alcoholic Charles Bukowski, distributed tattoo magazines and Beat literature, and arranged readings by writers like the late William Burroughs and Allen Ginsberg.

'Leonardo got a very alternative look at things early on,' says George DiCaprio. Three days after he was born,

novelist Hubert Selby Junior brought him a gift of a pair of tiny boxing gloves. Neighbours and frequent overnight guests were Harvey Pekar, R. Crumb and Bukowski. 'Leo was never excluded from open conversations about sex and drugs,' says his father, who maintains that, in addition to inheriting the 'DiCaprio power brows', his son also displays the family fearlessness: 'Leo is on a quest to find out how many things he can do in life and not do them straight. He would walk to the guillotine and act goofy.'

☆ Leo's first major big screen co-star, Robert De Niro, whom he claims he did not know until he auditioned for *This Boy's Life*.

grow up in a hippie family but you couldn't call us "apple pie" and Republican either,' he explains.

But at the same time his mother resembles any other. 'I can't see him as other people do', she says. 'All I am concerned about is his health – sleep more, exercise more, eat better. That's the litany. The rest? I wouldn't care if he gave up tomorrow.'

But Hollywood, the moneymen in black suits, the producers and directors and big name Oscar winners like Robert De Niro and Meryl Streep, have impressed on her that he is important, he is *that* talented. Peggy Farrar, his father's partner, who has been another great growing-up influence on Leonardo, is just as forthright. Her son Adam briefly paid his way through higher education by acting, so as well as living in the core of Hollywood she has witnessed the excesses and successes of the town, and of the business. She has seen the winners and losers and says of Leo, 'He's the golden boy. It all just comes to him.'

'They've convinced us', says Irmelin DiCaprio. And his father adds, 'He must have something. He gets all these film scripts every week.'

Both his parents work with him, in his own film production company.

It was different at school. I had a really tough time. I got mostly "B" grades.

With pot-smoking, rebel parents the youngster found he had little left to rebel against: 'Whatever I did would be something they'd already done. I mean, Dad would welcome it if I got a nose ring but I hate them. I'm afraid of leaving a hole in my face. Or having a tattoo and having to live with that stupid painting for the rest of my life. Why not just get a poster and put it up in your room?

'As far as my family are concerned, my parents were the rebellious ones – they're the people who have done everything and have nothing to prove. Anything I wanted to do in my life they would sort of allow. I didn't exactly

His mother has a boxed collection of tens of thousands of her son's fan letters stacked in every available space along with the piles of scripts read and not acted upon. 'I couldn't imagine working with anyone better,' she says. 'I'm in heaven. Whatever I was doing before [she was a legal secretary] wasn't as interesting as what's happening to Leonardo.'

The admiration goes both ways. 'I get along great with my parents,' says Leonardo. 'My Mom and Dad were separated before I could talk so I never knew anything different. I had a happy childhood – it's not a common occurrence in Hollywood. I'm an only child, which is very cool. I love it. I never missed having sisters and brothers in that way. My parents allowed me to do so much stuff I wanted.'

Inevitably there was a contrast between the regime at home and that at his schools, The Centre for Enriched

Studies and the John Marshall High School in Los Angeles. 'It was different at school. I had a really tough time. I got mostly "B" grades; I was never really much of a school person.

'I never got over the fact that we weren't allowed to learn what we wanted to learn. But then I asked myself why can't I just create a space for myself where I don't have to do math? Because I'm not good at it and if I have a problem with my taxes I'll get a tax man. I was frustrated. I wasn't happy learning things. I know it's up to you to a degree but a lot of times school is just so dull and boring: it's hard for a kid to learn in that environment. You got to school, you go to class, study this, study that, get your homework, go home. There's hardly any *vibrancy* there. I needed to get to a place where I was excited about learning.

'For me it's all about getting a person interested in a subject but linking a lot of happiness to it, a lot of *joy* in doing it. That was lacking for me – and maybe for a lot of kids in America.

☆ **Diane Keaton, who helped Leo to enjoy the laughter in their work....**

'I cheated a lot at school. It's a very unique art I think. It has to do with being aware of how the teacher is, first off, and seeing how much they take notice and the times that they do notice and the times that they don't notice and just pinpointing the times when they don't. I remember being hidden by other people's faces and having somebody next to you who you're friends with and is extremely smart.

'I have to commend this guy named Mustafa who probably helped me through three or four classes completely just because I sat next to him every time and I got to copy the homework right before class started. If I had problems on a test I'd just look over and Mustafa would show me his paper and I would write it down.

'You gotta know people and how they operate.

'I wasn't popular at school,' admits DiCaprio. 'What I would do in order to be more popular was put myself

15

on the line and joke around and be wacky and funny and I was always known as the wacky little kid. My Dad taught me not to be shy. I did impressions, all of it. I'd imitate people I'd just met who were interesting. I liked to become a character. Then I realized that that's not what I want to do. I didn't want to be a comedian to please other people.

'But I was good at impressions and still wanted to do them, to act them. One of my passions is to imitate people. My imitation of Michael Jackson is I think OK and everybody always gets a kick out of it, so much so that I wish I hadn't started doing it. It's not an obsession. It's just a ridiculous thing that I like to do that's funny. I started doing it one day when I was working on a movie

☆ Meryl Streep laughing at one of Leo's jokes.

☆ Revelations from Gwen Verdon in *Marvin's Room*.

16

(*Marvin's Room*, 1996) with Gwen Verdon and she says: "I taught Michael Jackson some moves for one of his TV specials." Then, she started doing this Michael Jackson dance thing – so she's cool.

'When I was a kid I used to do people I had seen on television like Charles Manson. I really had no idea who he was. I went to school and I was doing Manson with a swastika painted on my head. I got sent home. Then, my parents explained to me what Manson had done and I dropped him from my repertoire real quick.'

His father, who had lived through the terror days of the 1969 Manson family slayings of director Roman Polanski's pregnant wife Sharon Tate and five others in Hollywood, said his son's teachers were 'really alarmed' by the impersonations. 'I had to go to school and explain that it was an imitation – it was taken from something Leo had seen on television. He was acting it, not believing it.'

And that's how, mostly, he's dealing with his fame. He accepts that for many his life must be a dream: 'I'm out of school, making a lot of money, doing a lot of movies, can do anything, meet anyone, go anywhere, date anyone, buy anything ...' He credits Irmelin with keeping his feet on the ground: 'My mother is a good leveller. She keeps herself very separate from all the glitz and glamour of the business. She gives me advice and keeps reminding me that acting is a just a job.

'She has about the same enthusiasm for what I do as if I worked in a convenience store.'

But it's not quite the same. Especially when your son is being flagged by

every power in Hollywood as *the* movie star of the times.

He has been asked to star in a film biography of James Dean – an immortal example of a business which not only eats its young but feeds off their memory. It is a project that Warner Brothers studios have been trying to pull together since 1995. Nothing is set but DiCaprio is a fan of James Dean as well as of several other charismatic and paradoxical movie legends:

'I love Montgomery Clift. I think that he possessed a lot. Of course, there's Brando, but I think Montgomery Clift was an actor that really, you know, was able to make you feel for him more than anybody else at the time.

'I've watched a lot of old movies and there's sort of a different way of acting. I mean, it's this leading man sort of thing where you have your composure. Montgomery Clift was all over the place and you felt he was on the verge of tears all the time. He was the only actor that really got me to say: "Oh, boy, what's ... you know, what's wrong?"

'And James Dean too. I really love James Dean's performances. I've always thought he really had a lot of good stuff going ...

I can do anything, meet anyone, go anywhere, date anyone, buy anything ...

GROWING PAINS

"THEY WANTED TO CHANGE ME INTO WHITE BREAD"
LEONARDO DiCAPRIO
1997

There's no home ground advantage to getting work in Hollywood by being born there. For every couple of thousand local kids looking for a television or movie 'break' there are just as many arriving in town every week – some with parents, portfolios and agents in tow.

DiCaprio seems to have made it his short life's work to be *cool*. At the age of six he arranged to attend a public audition for a commercial agency, a routine Hollywood 'cattle call'. Years later he still remembers his motives. 'I decided I wanted to be an actor so I could be cool and all the girls could see me.

'At this agency a bunch of us kids were lined up and we were just like cattle – even then I realized why they talk about them as "cattle calls". You're just a number on a list. This woman is there and she goes: "I'll take you and the rest of you are out."

'I was broken-hearted, so I went up to her and asked why she hadn't picked me. "Wrong haircut" is all she said.'

But you can't keep an ambitious and cool six-year-old down. He thinks he was about nine years old when he got an agent. 'This lady took me on and changed my name. Leonardo DiCaprio was "too ethnic". I got changed into something more white-bread so I could go

to auditions and say: "Look, I'm Lenny Williams – and I have blond hair." That really wasn't my scene – I got out of that as I got older. I like my name even though in school they would call me "Leonardo Retardo."'

He was all of an ageing fourteen when he found an agent who wasn't fazed by his name. Just his talent. Even then the potential was showing. 'I became really serious about acting then. Up till that time I was too involved in being a kid.' DiCaprio will tell you now that acting is a serious and important part of his life and, although he acts his age (and younger sometimes, perhaps recapturing some of the teenage years that went into the movies), it is what he is committed to. For a lifetime.

Early on he was seeing dollar bills, easy money, although he qualifies his financial yearnings: 'I always wanted to be an actor, ever since I was very young. I was always acting, you know, goofing around and doing funny things with my friends. I always knew that's what I wanted to do and my brother (Peggy Farrar's son Adam) started off and he made like 50,000 dollars from this whole thing. I said: "Oh, my God, 50,000 dollars." It was a Golden Grahams thing, a commercial for cookies!

'I was eleven years old. I thought I could live off that for the rest of my life. You know, that's great, you know. That kept on being my driving force. I said to myself that

☆ The young, moody and magnificent Leo.

I thought I could live off that for the rest of my life. I could act *and* make money so I started getting into it when I was, like, just thirteen years old.'

His mother took him to auditions, while his father went through scripts. He landed a role in a commercial advertising 'Matchbox' toy cars and then went on to appear in dozens of others, one of which was a Walt Disney production entitled *Mickey's Safety Club*. Another, in 1989, was a US Government Public Awareness TV spot titled *How to Deal with a Parent who Takes Drugs*.

'You wouldn't think that would be a career booster,' he says with an enormous smile. But of course, it was.

In the late 1980s and early 1990s, American television was dominated by situation comedies aimed at 'family' audiences. This was not with the wellbeing of the nation in mind, simply a commercial ploy to tempt the biggest audience. DiCaprio made his TV début in the daddy of all family shows, a Saturday morning revival of the classic *Lassie* series, which had begun so many years before on the big screen with child star Elizabeth Taylor in *Lassie Come Home*.

He was good. He knew his lines, turned up on time and there were never any problems. He was a professional in a field where, for casting agents, young age and pressuring parents can cancel out talent. DiCaprio got the work, often against competition from several hundred other just as 'pretty' young actors. 'He just had that something extra,' explains casting agent Marvin Hayfield.

He played the sought-after 'motivation character' of a teenage alcoholic in the NBC TV popular daytime soap opera *Santa Barbara*. In 1990 he got a 'guest star' top slot in the prime time series *The Outsiders*. The same year he landed a role in the short-lived *Parenthood* (which spelled out the demographics it was after in the title). He played the family's eldest son Garry. More high profile was *Growing Pains*, which had made a teen idol out of star Kirk Cameron, who was only fifteen when the show began in 1985.

When DiCaprio joined the series it was an established if syrupy hit. Now DiCaprio shyly admits, 'That show was sort of embarrassing'. It revolved around the Seaver family: Joanna Kerns as the mother had returned to work as a local newspaper reporter while Alan Thicke as the psychiatrist father moved his practice into their home to better raise the children. Social messages – preaching, according to some critics – were mixed with the set-up comedy situations. Before he found fame and *Friends*, Matthew Perry played a regular character who died in a drink-driving-focused episode. DiCaprio joined the regular cast as Luke, a homeless boy. The show's fan mail soared – he was the 'cute kid', the urchin that everyone wanted to 'mother'.

☆ **No place to hide – 'lost Leo' in** *This Boy's Life.*

It was his first experience of being a showbusiness pin-up, although many of his fans were even younger than he was then. 'It was a good experience for me in that I got to know what I don't want to do. I had these lame lines ... I couldn't bear it actually. But everyone was bright and chipper. Kirk gave me a lesson in the Bible. He gave me a constant positive perspective on life.

'I learned a lot from Alan Thicke, including how to put the moves on women.

'I'd rather people didn't write that I was on the show but you get started with whatever is available and you stick with it until somebody realizes: "Hey, this kid can really act."'

The producers of *Critters 3* – a beastly thing about nasty humanity-threatening creatures – weren't looking for Olivier when they cast DiCaprio in their straight-to-

video horror. When heavily pressured into even recalling that movie, all he will say is: 'It was experience.'

Not, apparently, a good one.

But like the television work it helped get him noticed. He was still that cute youngster with flyaway hair hanging over his left eye – boyish looks with a boy's figure. Everywhere people told him, 'You look like River Phoenix,' or 'Aren't you that blond kid on the soap?' or, worse still, 'You're going to be the next Johnny Depp.'

All the growing pains of an early career, but he was indeed 'cute' enough to be able to avoid grasping and exploitative agents. 'I told myself I wanted to be myself and act the way *I* act not the way somebody else acts. But you get labelled. I said I was going to do my own

thing and not try to be hunk of the month. There was no future in that. Hollywood likes to give people titles, to call you the next whatever ...'

By 1992 he was close to completing his high school education with a home tutor. 'Life', he said preciously that year, 'is my college now.' But it was not to be. It was Oscar winner Robert De Niro who was to take on the role of Leo's teacher.

British film director Michael Caton-Jones who had helped guide another young star, Michael J. Fox, from television to the movies in *Doc Hollywood*, and who had had great success directing Jessica Lange and Liam Neeson in *Rob Roy*, was casting a much more intimate movie for release in 1993.

This Boy's Life was author Tobias Wolff's moving story of his own upbringing in late 1950s America. It was the time of the American Dream of the Cadillac, the television and the white picket fence – the simple good life. Everyone wanted the same; it was not a decade in which to be different.

The book – and the movie – tell the story of nuclear family life with a twist – the twist being Tobias Wolff, who so wanted to be good but somehow couldn't achieve it without being bad. Wolff's autobiographical story focuses on his mother's marriage to Dwight Hansen, a mean-spirited control freak. He moves the family to the symbolically named town of Concrete. Only 'Dysfunctional' would have been a name more apt.

'Toby was a little snot who needed someone to be strict,' says DiCaprio, quickly adding, 'but he didn't need a maniac like his stepfather Dwight. Dwight took the strictness to another level.'

In the movie, DiCaprio's Toby is first seen driving to Utah with his overly-optimistic mother Caroline (played by the engaging Ellen Barkin) who's running from an abusive boyfriend in Florida. There's a mix-up, the boyfriend catches up, they escape again to Seattle only because that bus leaves before the one to Arizona. Enter the Pacific Northwest and Dwight played by Robert De

Niro at his chilling, though often darkly humorous, best.

Caroline marries him, mainly in the hope that a new family will calm DiCaprio's Toby who is shedding puberty for delinquency. Dwight is hail-fellow-well-met until he has a drink and then his veneer of awkward goodwill gives way to the bully beneath. He regards Toby as a rival for his new wife's affection. He inflicts damage not so

I said I was going to do my own thing and not try to be hunk of the month.

☆ Short back and sides.

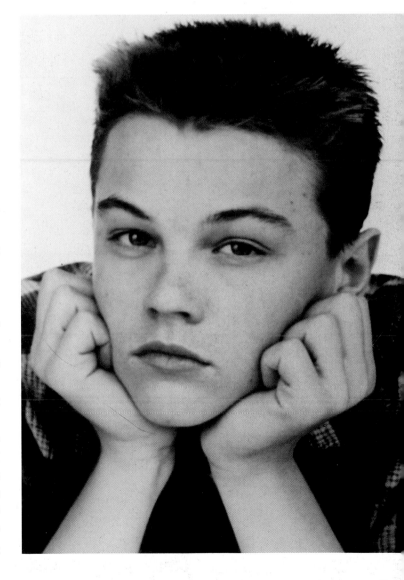

☆ **Young man in the making...the growing Leo.**

much physically as mentally as he stomps around in a scoutmaster's uniform, a military-style thuggish, self-loathing man. Of course, Toby hates his stepfather.

DiCaprio's performance won great praise: 'astonishing', said *Newsweek* magazine; America's *US Magazine* raved: 'Playing against De Niro, DiCaprio more than holds his own'; *The New York Daily News* declared: 'This is the breakthrough performance of the decade ...'

'Moving, smart and made with passion,' is how *Newsweek* summed up the film. Michael Caton-Jones gave this verdict on his young star: 'He has this amazing ability to convey quite complex emotions. All I wanted him to do was be a kid. He did that magnificently. And all the rest ...' Many critics believe DiCaprio pulled a felony and stole the movie from De Niro, as easy as that supermarket bubblegum.

DiCaprio says he was helped by his 'immediate connection' with the British director for whom he auditioned seven times. 'I got the part by just going in and doing it, no mumbo jumbo. I didn't worry what De Niro thought. I went in, looked him in the eye, and got the part. I was confident even though I'd never done anything like it before. Now, I realize it was ignorant confidence. I had no idea.'

What's more, many of the scenes, including a fight with De Niro's Dwight, were draining. 'I got a couple of bruises from big old Bobby D. But he was very careful and nice about it. People say things about him, that he stays in character between scenes. He didn't stay in character with me. He was really nice and considerate. He said to me: "You did the most honest portrayal of the hundred people we tested for the role. You didn't have a lot of the mannerisms kids have today." You get emotionally distraught doing scenes like that. But you know it's acting and you know the pain is temporary and film is forever.'

The De Niro influence in that philosophy is plain to see, and the Oscar-winning actor says he felt a paternal pull towards DiCaprio. 'I'm used to certain things I feel as a father and in *This Boy's Life* I used them for Leonardo. He's about the same age as my own son and, you know,

☆ **Young man in the making...the growing Leo.**

much physically as mentally as he stomps around in a scoutmaster's uniform, a military-style thuggish, self-loathing man. Of course, Toby hates his stepfather.

DiCaprio's performance won great praise: 'astonishing', said *Newsweek* magazine; America's *US Magazine* raved: 'Playing against De Niro, DiCaprio more than holds his own'; *The New York Daily News* declared: 'This is the breakthrough performance of the decade ...'

'Moving, smart and made with passion,' is how *Newsweek* summed up the film. Michael Caton-Jones gave this verdict on his young star: 'He has this amazing ability to convey quite complex emotions. All I wanted him to do was be a kid. He did that magnificently. And all the rest ...' Many critics believe DiCaprio pulled a felony and stole the movie from De Niro, as easy as that supermarket bubblegum.

DiCaprio says he was helped by his 'immediate connection' with the British director for whom he auditioned seven times. 'I got the part by just going in and doing it, no mumbo jumbo. I didn't worry what De Niro thought. I went in, looked him in the eye, and got the part. I was confident even though I'd never done anything like it before. Now, I realize it was ignorant confidence. I had no idea.'

What's more, many of the scenes, including a fight with De Niro's Dwight, were draining. 'I got a couple of bruises from big old Bobby D. But he was very careful and nice about it. People say things about him, that he stays in character between scenes. He didn't stay in character with me. He was really nice and considerate. He said to me: "You did the most honest portrayal of the hundred people we tested for the role. You didn't have a lot of the mannerisms kids have today." You get emotionally distraught doing scenes like that. But you know it's acting and you know the pain is temporary and film is forever.'

The De Niro influence in that philosophy is plain to see, and the Oscar-winning actor says he felt a paternal pull towards DiCaprio. 'I'm used to certain things I feel as a father and in *This Boy's Life* I used them for Leonardo. He's about the same age as my own son and, you know, thing and not try to be hunk of the month. There was no future in that. Hollywood likes to give people titles, to call you the next whatever ...'

By 1992 he was close to completing his high school education with a home tutor. 'Life', he said preciously that year, 'is my college now.' But it was not to be. It was Oscar winner Robert De Niro who was to take on the role of Leo's teacher.

British film director Michael Caton-Jones who had helped guide another young star, Michael J. Fox, from television to the movies in *Doc Hollywood*, and who had had great success directing Jessica Lange and Liam Neeson in *Rob Roy*, was casting a much more intimate movie for release in 1993.

This Boy's Life was author Tobias Wolff's moving story of his own upbringing in late 1950s America. It was the time of the American Dream of the Cadillac, the television and the white picket fence – the simple good life. Everyone wanted the same; it was not a decade in which to be different.

The book – and the movie – tell the story of nuclear family life with a twist – the twist being Tobias Wolff, who so wanted to be good but somehow couldn't achieve it without being bad. Wolff's autobiographical story focuses on his mother's marriage to Dwight Hansen, a mean-spirited control freak. He moves the family to the symbolically named town of Concrete. Only 'Dysfunctional' would have been a name more apt.

'Toby was a little snot who needed someone to be strict,' says DiCaprio, quickly adding, 'but he didn't need a maniac like his stepfather Dwight. Dwight took the strictness to another level.'

In the movie, DiCaprio's Toby is first seen driving to Utah with his overly-optimistic mother Caroline (played by the engaging Ellen Barkin) who's running from an abusive boyfriend in Florida. There's a mix-up, the boyfriend catches up, they escape again to Seattle only because that bus leaves before the one to Arizona. Enter the Pacific Northwest and Dwight played by Robert De

Niro at his chilling, though often darkly humorous, best.

Caroline marries him, mainly in the hope that a new family will calm DiCaprio's Toby who is shedding puberty for delinquency. Dwight is hail-fellow-well-met until he has a drink and then his veneer of awkward goodwill gives way to the bully beneath. He regards Toby as a rival for his new wife's affection. He inflicts damage not so

I said I was going to do my own thing and not try to be hunk of the month.

☆ Short back and sides.

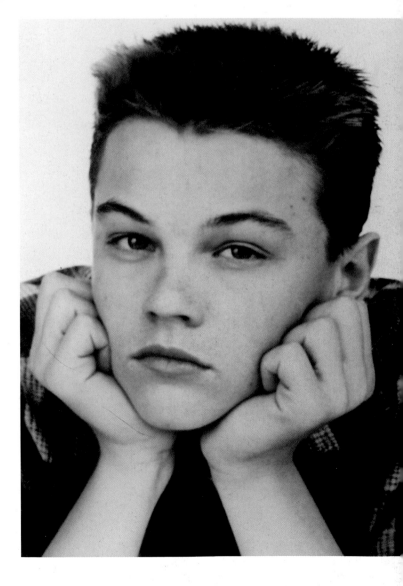

☆ Trouble on the horizon.

sometimes I want to kill my son so that just transfers to poor Leonardo ... Being a father is being a father. A father knows what the experience is. Leonardo knew how to handle the situations   he could act himself out of every problem on the set. He was a natural, a joy to work with. He connected with me and the director. Especially Michael, who was very good. Ellen liked the kid too and helped him a lot.'

But one thing that 'The Method' style of acting could not control was DiCaprio's body – it grew and grew, just like Topsy. They say that some actors really grow up in the movies. Leonardo DiCaprio did – by four inches, and was forced to crouch in some scenes to appear shorter than De Niro. DiCaprio takes a philosophical view, 'Height doesn't matter. It's all in the performance'. In the same way, he is unfazed by working with screen legend De Niro. 'A lot of times, acting is getting rid of precon-ceived ideas about what the character should do and just doing it. I told myself I wasn't starring with a legend. I wanted to think of him not as De Niro, but as Dwight, this schmucky guy from up north that I was smarter than.

'It was not so much a story about an abused kid as a more beautiful story about a boy growing up, becoming a man, coming to terms with his manhood, but having to deal with somebody who wants to control his life. It's about how he deals with that situation, how he doesn't let it hinder him as far as his life goes. It didn't take a lot of research.

'If I'm sitting there and Robert De Niro with his mug in my face is just screaming at me I'm going to feel scared and intimidated. I just let it happen naturally as far as those moments went.

'Just acting with De Niro you learn the tricks of the trade. I learned a lot, including how film works and the beauty of being subtle and how that works. Especially if you are a main character.

'De Niro is kinda like a god for every-body and people ask me what advice he gave me but ... The first scene I had with

I told myself I wasn't starring with a legend.

him in *This Boy's Life* he was cutting off my hair. I just sat there and I was a bit scared, and I just sort of made that scared face. I knew it was going to be a short scene so I wanted to relax before I did anything drastic. And he went with me all the time.

'And the haircut! You know, people say to me: "Wasn't it ridiculous having those hair-styles back then?" And I think what about some of the things we're doing now? Hello? Ten years from now we're going to be thinking: "Oh my Gawd, how *could* they have their hair like that? And, like that ducktail or whatnot, it's just a

My mother has a young attitude and is very free about things.

☆ At last, the Hollywood Hunk!

passing fad. Just like life, you know. For the movie it made it true to the time, the haircut did that. It made him and his friends just like Elvis, like Elvis impersonators. But bad ones. He and his friends were trying to be cool – we're all always trying to be cool in our way – and at the end he grows up and he is almost that rebel type because he's really going through it. He's an angered teen. All teens are angered. He's almost a James Dean character at the end. Anguished.

'And with that haircut you would be too!' he laughs.

De Niro's Scout uniform was not up to his usual Armani threads either. But looks, of course, weren't everything. 'Of course, he's one of the best American actors alive and I admire the guy so much,' enthuses DiCaprio. 'So many people around the world do. Doing that film with him was important but it wasn't about an actor working with Robert De Niro. It's a boy growing up with an intimidating character like Dwight in his life. I couldn't think of him as a boy working with De Niro. I had to think of a lowly guy from Concrete who was just depressed about life and deal with him. I couldn't be fascinated with working with Robert De Niro so I got over that. I got over that quickly.

'I was put in an environment where I was the lead character in a film opposite Robert De Niro and Ellen Barkin and I had to sort of maintain not thinking about that. Otherwise, I would have got freaked out. I think I'm most proud of that film and part of the reason is because it was my first film.

'My mother loved the movie – that was why the Ellen Barkin character was so important. It showed the freedom they had, like my mom and I. They're two kids roaming at the beginning of the picture: they had a best-friends relationship. My mother, she's a great mom. Very cool. My mother has a young attitude and is very free about things.'

He learned much about using his emotions, suspending reality, from his screen 'mom', Ellen Barkin, the former wife of Irish actor Gabriel Byrne who four years later he would be working with in Paris. 'She was supportive. She really taught me a lot. She had lived her life in the movies – she had gone through good and bad times – and it was an education working with her. Just think of the people she had been in movies with: Jack Nicholson! Al Pacino! Jeff Bridges! Dennis Quaid! Robert De Niro! Me!! And lots more.'

☆ **Tall and moody, Leo struts for the camera.**

Whether DiCaprio perceived her as saint or sinner all the evidence suggests Ellen Barkin could be perfectly cast as Ms Capability, a mistress of control and probably anyone she cared to fancy. The flagrant body language says it loud and clear before there's a hint of conversation. Professionally, she's proved herself opposite the major leading men of her generation. Personally, she's coped with divorce from Gabriel Byrne, the life of a busy single mum to their two young children, and with being the subject of romantic speculation over just about every man that she meets.

Her raunchy love scenes with Pacino in *Sea of Love* are part of Hollywood lore, likened to the classic Lana Turner/John Garfield clinches of the original *The Postman Always Knocks Twice*. As much as De Niro, Barkin is a Hollywood veteran, with plenty of ideas about the business for the young DiCaprio to mull over.

'I'm not somebody who wants to be given a job that I don't know how to do,' says Barkin. 'I would feel really shitty about myself. I studied for several years before I went to work. It had been drilled into my head what a horrible job it was – the hard knocks, rejection, bad feelings – so I thought if I was going to have to swallow that for the rest of my life I wasn't going to go home and say: "And I don't even know what I'm doing." '

'I've made a lot of wonderful films that haven't made a dime but they were good movies. Sometimes I'll run with the Hollywood pack and sometimes I won't. I will continue to take jobs I want to take. If it works out for my career then I've gotten lucky.

'Bobby and I both told Leo that the important thing is to work but then, when the works starts coming in, to choose carefully. To be clever, not greedy. And, my God, it is a temptation when you've been waiting tables to take the big money, what seems to be the easy money.

'My work is a safety valve. I'd rather my characters made mistakes than I did. I think it's important for me not to judge the characters I play and say: "I'm a mother so I only want to play a good mother." That's not so interesting. It's fascinating for me to explore the aspect of motherhood that is not positive, where you make mistakes. You know, people mess up at certain points of

their lives and at different points of my life I'm interested in exploring the people who mess up.

'You learn from that and you can pass on the lesson to your kids and other youngsters.'

DiCaprio listened to her life classes – on and off the set of *This Boy's Life* – but admits that even after the film, and his much-applauded performance, he was still not sure 'where I wanted to go as an actor'. He says his indecision was not helped by the film, which, true to life, was veiled with shades and produced no black and white answers: 'I like movies that you can't describe and *This Boy's Life* was one.

'You can't just say it was only about a boy growing up with a mean stepfather. You have to tell about the other side of Dwight – the side that did help Toby straighten out.

'You have to tell about Toby's homosexual best friend [the wonderful Jonah Blechman]. You have to tell why Toby hangs out with idiots and gets drunk. Nothing is simple, nothing is clear cut. Movies that are like life work better for me. I think they work better for most people.

'There are a lot of people who have gotten good roles at a young age and their careers later slopped out. Meaning no disrespect to anybody, I wanted to hold out for what I believed were good projects. I set some standards and hoped ...

'I respect the gift, but acting is not the biggest deal in the world. If the gift means disaster, I won't go there.

'There's some odd situations sometimes but everyone sort of endures – it's a small price to pay for the kind of work I'm getting to do.'

☆ **The look that launched a thousand film offers.**

☆ The eyes, like blinds, disguise his inner thoughts.

OSCAR BOY

"I'VE GOT TO TURN INTO A MAN. THERE ARE A LOT MORE ROLES FOR YOUNG MEN THAN OLD TEENAGERS"
LEONARDO DiCAPRIO 1993

The air-conditioning inside the Viper Room on Sunset Boulevard works much better than anywhere else in the serried ranks of bungalows in East Hollywood. The club, which is co-owned by Johnny Depp, is a magnet for the tourists and the autograph hunters and, in a perverse sort of way, for the stars who want to avoid them.

There is no sign to announce the location of the Viper Room. Patrons just *know* it's there. Depp oversees the music, an eclectic mix from Johnny Cash to Oasis or Iggy Pop. Cash has made personal appearances as has gonzo journalist Hunter S. Thompson.

River Phoenix was a regular until he died from a drug overdose at 8825 Sunset, collapsing on the pavement outside the Viper Room. You can see the spot on the security video monitor above the bar.

'It was a fucking wake-up call for everybody for sure', says Depp, adding with a sneer, 'They tried to drag me through the mud. They tried to drag the club through the mud. But I don't give a fuck what the tabloid press writes. Forget about me. Forget about the club. The club is going to go away at some point. It's just a piece of real estate. But to drag River's name through the mud and turn the incident into a fucking circus was such a horrible thing. It was unbelievable.'

Early in the evening that River Phoenix died, Leonardo DiCaprio was at a Hallowe'enparty 'It was at the house of these twin actors and I remember it was dark and everyone was drunk and I was passing through crowds of people so thick it was almost like two lanes of traffic.

'I glanced at a guy in a mask and I suddenly knew that it was River Phoenix. I wanted to reach out and say "hello" because he was this great mystery and we'd never met and I thought he probably wouldn't blow me off because I'd done stuff by then that was probably worth watching.

'Then I got stuck in a lane of traffic and slid right past him. The next thing I knew River Phoenix was dead. The same night.

'With River it's sad but I don't know if it was the effects of the business or his life.'

Phoenix, whose parents, like DiCaprio's, were 1960s rebels, and commune-style bohemians, was at first an unlikely candidate to have died young, aged twenty-three, from drug abuse. But Phoenix, who wore the 'new James Dean' label, was not the anti-drug, pro-environment, clean-living star he seemed. After his death it became clear that he had more than dabbled in drugs including 'Belushis' – heroin and cocaine mixed 'speedballs' named after 'Blues Brother' John Belushi who died

☆ Those teeth, those eyes, THAT shirt.

after being injected with them. The shock of the sudden death provoked an anti-Hollywood, anti-drug campaign.

Somehow, DiCaprio, young, talented and the 'new, new James Dean', was associated with the drug death of River Phoenix and with the nihilistic Los Angeles club and drug scene. By now he was acutely aware of all the perils out there in the real world. Actress Tracey Gold who had worked with him on *Growing Pains* had been a victim of eating disorders. The offices of Madonna's favoured paediatrician Paul Fleiss were close to where he grew up and the doctor's daughter Heidi Fleiss had become infamous as a Hollywood madam supplying call girls to the stars.

The connections were happenstance, but for the gossip pages circumstantial evidence is frequently more than enough.

If you were young and gifted then you just *had* to be wild.

There were stories and then more stories. 'He seldom sleeps, so intense is his partying', wrote the ageing New York columnist Liz Smith. He was linked with actress Juliette Lewis who had exploded onto the scene as De Niro's young victim in *Cape Fear* and as Mallory in Oliver Stone's controversial *Natural Born Killers*. Indeed they were linked, in the movies. The two were starring with Johnny Depp in what was to be DiCaprio's breakthrough movie, his star-making vehicle, the wonderfully moving *What's Eating Gilbert Grape?*

DiCaprio can capture it all in a couple of sentences. 'It's about Johnny Depp in this small town and his mother,

☆ **How many millions for those dreams?**

☆ A hat trick of stars: Leo with Juliette Lewis and Johnny Depp.

who weighs about 400 pounds, his retarded brother, me, his friend, Crispin Glover, his girlfriend, Juliette Lewis and his married lover, Mary Steenburgen.

'He's slowly flipping out. Things break down. You can't simply say it's about this or it's about that.'

It was certainly a tangled plot. As was DiCaprio's route to working with Depp, who with girlfriend Kate Moss, comprised the supercool on-and-off couple of the 1990s, the hip transatlantic package.

At first, he was planning to work with the onetime hipster and gay icon, Bette Midler. The film was *Hocus Pocus* and was intended as a lively comedy in which Midler, Sarah Jessica Parker and Rosie O' Donnell played three witches. 'I didn't know then the type of movies I wanted to do. I just felt like doing a movie is doing a movie.

'I get money and fame and that's great and I can have some fun. And I was up for *Hocus Pocus* and I knew it was awful but it was just like: "OK, they're offering me more and more money. Isn't that what you do? You do movies and you get more money." But something inside me kept saying: "Don't do this movie."

'And everyone around me was saying: "Leonardo, how could you not take a movie?" And I said to myself: "OK, I'll audition for this movie *Gilbert Grape* and if I don't get that I'll do *Hocus Pocus*."

'I found myself working so hard, investing so much time and energy in *Gilbert Grape*, that I finally got it and

Things break down. You can't simply say it's about this or it's about that.

35

☆ In character: Leo in his breakthrough movie Gilbert Grape.

With performing I'm like the scorpion in the story...

it was like such a weight off my shoulders.'

It won him an Oscar nomination. And saved him from *Hocus Pocus* which was one of the box office bombs of 1993. Instead, he shone in *Gilbert Grape*, which, he says, was a 'fantastic experience' adding, 'With performing I'm like the scorpion in the story, the one where he stings the frog who is taking him across the pond even though it means they're both gonna die – it's something in my nature.'

The scorpion tale is, we can imagine, an allegory which Depp and DiCaprio would have discussed. Depp is a decade older. He has been through the early fame game – and the drugs and drink. 'I experimented, especially when I was a kid,' he admits. 'A few drinks have had me. It's just kind of point-less. I mean some people can drink – you know, a few whiskeys or vodkas. But I just keep going. Many of my characters carry sadness – Gilbert Grape did.

'Man, yeah, Johnny was unhappy then,' Depp adds ruefully. 'It was a pretty dark time for me. I don't know what was going on. I was poisoning myself beyond belief. There was a lot of liquor, a lot of liquor. I was in a pretty unhealthy state. It was a very sad time for me. I can't watch *Gilbert Grape*. We chase our tails for so long. Getting high is about fucking trying to numb something; getting loaded and trying to destroy your life. Well, you just get to a point and you go: "Fuck! What am I doing to myself?"

☆ 'Things break down. You can't simply say it's about this or that.' DiCaprio on *Gilbert Grape*.

ALBERT
GRAPE

AUG. 22. 1938
OCT. 13. 1978

'It's not so much redemption as it is clarity. This really shows I'm getting older. I'm sounding like John Denver or something. I look forward to having peace of mind. I know that we all get there eventually but it entails, at least for me, going through a lot of chaos.'

River Phoenix. The Viper Room. The legendary Johnny Depp. It was an important close-up for DiCaprio of the 'Young Hollywood' life.

For the moment, though, he was more interested in getting his role as Grape's retarded brother just right. 'It wasn't until I went to a home for kids who were mentally disabled that I could perfect the character. I interviewed about twenty different kids with different disabilities and I spent a couple of hours with them. I tape recorded them, and when I listened to the tapes I tried to pick out each little thing to

The greatest challenge was to stay always in character.

incorporate into the character. It changed my whole idea about mentally disabled people. You think you're going to be talking to them and they'll be all over the place but they were interested in me and why I was there. They seemed to understand – I just wanted to talk to them more. It was like speaking with children with adult characteristics, although their minds work in a different way to anyone else's. Strangely, they don't have a lot to worry about. Grasping their special freedom was the important thing for the role.' Research or no research, it was a difficult part. As DiCaprio sums up, 'The greatest challenge was to stay always in character. It was like continual improvisation class.'

But DiCaprio graduated with honours. In a roundup of the best films of 1993 the respected screenwriter William Goldman – fabulously famous since 1969's *Butch Cassidy and the Sundance Kid* – wrote: 'Please don't anything bad *ever* happen to Leonardo DiCaprio.'

In the film, from Peter Hedges' first novel, DiCaprio's Arnie is turning 18, even though he wasn't meant to live past childhood. He's a problem for his obese mother who hasn't gone out in seven years, perhaps since Dad hanged himself in the cellar. Arnie, who Gilbert is supposed to be looking after, keeps climbing the water tower when no one's looking and the police are getting fed up with it. Gilbert and Arnie are locked in a convincing relationship of love and frustration.

DiCaprio wore a mouthpiece to give Arnie a slight visible oddness, but under the tender direction of Lasse Hallstrom – responsible for the Swedish cult classic *My Life as a Dog* – he plays the mentally-disabled teenager superbly. Employing incredible insight and compassion as well as an array of ticks and twitches, the performance tiptoes around hysteria. American critic John Anderson thought that Dustin Hoffman's performance as an idiot savant in *Rain Man* was 'a party trick by comparison to DiCaprio as Arnie Grape.' Janet Maslin in the *New York Times* commented: 'He winds up capturing the enormous range of Arnie's emotions and making it clear why the Grape brothers share such an unbreakable bond. The performance has a sharp, desperate intensity from beginning to end.'

The young actor had presented a picture of mental retardation that was joyful rather than pitiful. Hollywood loved it. Really loved it.

Soon he found himself invited to address a big audience – more than one billion people watching the Academy Awards. He received a Best Supporting Actor nomination for *Gilbert Grape*. He knew he had arrived and that his graduation from the 'embarrassing' roles of his teenage years was complete. He joked at the time, 'Funny, I thought that on my gravestone they were going to write: "This is the guy from *Growing Pains*." I guess this will change that.' Nevertheless, those roles had provided the young DiCaprio with invaluable experience and versatility. As Marcia Ross, who can claim to have 'discovered' DiCaprio when she cast him in *Parenthood*, points out: 'The great actors – and he'll be acknowledged as one – can do lots of roles. I believe he should try everything.'

Being an Oscar nominee was a tough new role for him. 'The Academy Awards was a big burden for me because of my problem with speaking in front of big audiences. I do much better with it now but back then it

☆ On the promotional beat: posing at the Beverly Hilton Hotel.

☆ Leo The Grin.

was this gut-wrenching fear of slipping up and doing something horrible ...In front of three billion people.

'Or crying or doing something that's embarrassing. I'm such a critical person of other people; when I watch people who do that I go: "Oh, what a fuckin' idiot." And I put that pressure on myself. So I was dreading winning. It was like this weight on my shoulders for so long and there were so many people who were saying: "Hey, you might have a chance." And I was saying: "No, no, no. I'm not going to win."

'And all the time I was convincing myself and I said to myself: "I'm not gonna plan a speech because I'm not gonna win."

'I invited my Mom and Dad and Peggy Farrar. I was so nervous and when I get nervous my palms start to sweat and I just start to twitch, sort of like an animal. And then I came to the Awards and people started telling me: "Hey, you gotta pretty good chance of winning tonight."

'And this thing started to consume me and I started shaking in my seat and still having this poised smile and inside being petrified.

'Mine was the first one up and my mom had to go to the bathroom. And they announced: "The nominees for Best Supporting Actor are ..." And my mom wasn't there! And I knew if my mom wasn't there it would be terrible. I saw this guard holding my mom back. She was trying to jump through a bunch of people and they showed the first person: "Tommy Lee Jones in *The Fugitive* ..."

'I knew I had to do something. My Mom *had* to be next to me. So I turned to the security guards and I mouthed: "Let her fucking in." And the guy looks at me and I said: "I'm a nominee." I never do that kind of shit but I figured this was really important.

'And my mom just scooted in and jumped in the seat and like, in five seconds, she adjusted herself. I adjusted myself and was sitting there with a smile on my face like "Aw, Gawd, this is great." Meanwhile, I'm just about ready to die.

'And when they announced that Tommy Lee Jones had won I wanted to get down on the ground and thank God. Nobody was happier for him than me, and that's the fucking truth.'

Despite not winning, the nomination had moved the young actor into a higher Hollywood league, where the rewards – and pitfalls – of success were much greater than anything he had experienced before. But by now DiCaprio has worked with the big stars and is aware of the menace, as well as the pleasures of superstardom: 'I've changed. You can't help it. Your mind starts working in a different way. You feel really scrutinized by people. I know what I have to do so people will like me but I try to avoid being phoney. If I notice myself doing something just to please somebody else, I stop it. When I'm aware of it that is – sometimes you do it and don't even *know* you're doing it – and that's scary.

'At the end of the day I know I've had more fun being famous than I would have had otherwise.' DiCaprio smiles. 'The attention I'm getting, having people I respect admire me – it's not bad for a kid from East Hollywood! I've always been spontaneous and outgoing. Having fun is a huge priority for me – whatever gets said or written about it.

'I know where the line is and when not to go over it.

'It's like the standards I want to keep in my work. They make people out to be pieces of meat, and there's a new side of beef each month. I'd like to stick to roles and movies that are high quality whatever the age I'm playing. There's a lot more roles for young men than for old teenagers.'

Especially when Sharon Stone rides into town.

I know where the line is and when not to go over it.

KISS THE GIRLS

"HE'S SO GOOD IT'S SCARY...
I WAS DYING TO HAVE HIM..."
SHARON STONE
ON LEONARDO DiCAPRIO, 1997

After the Oscar success of Kevin Costner's *Dances With Wolves* and Clint Eastwood's *Unforgiven*, Westerns rode back into Hollywood. Sharon Stone, who with *Basic Instinct* had become Hollywood's most sensational leading lady, saw a trend and decided that she should co-produce a Western with herself as the starring protagonist.

In 1992 Carolco had planned to pay the then number one movie lady, *Pretty Woman* Julia Roberts, $7 million for a similar adventure movie called *The Revengers*. Stone was now getting the same sort of money – plus percentage profit 'points'.

The Quick and the Dead was backed by Tri-Star Pictures – the distributors of *Basic Instinct*. Stone was working with people she knew. The new film was eagerly anticipated as one of the major blockbuster films of 1994–5. Stone realized this instantly and went into her control mode.

British moviemaker and screenwriter Simon Moore's script for *The Quick and the Dead* began to be offered for sale in Hollywood in 1993. Moore, who wrote and directed the English thriller *Under Suspicion* starring Liam Neeson and the UK television series *Traffick*, wanted to make the film himself. That is, produce and direct it. Sharon Stone wanted things her way, and was willing to pay for it.

One million dollars to Moore.

After she had read the script about a tough Wild West woman out to revenge the death of her father, a story packed with a motley assortment of characters with names like Fly, Flatnose, Ratsy, Ace, Kid and Herod, she couldn't resist. Sharon Stone, who had waited all those years for stardom, was determined to blow away all of the opposition.

Simon Moore had wanted to direct his screenplay. But Stone wanted the former music video maker Sam Raimi who had directed the chilling *Darkman* and *Army of Darkness* for the big screen. She had done her research. She knew what she wanted. She had the script, the vehicle literally to ride on from *Basic Instinct*, and she wanted Raimi. The only hurdle was the North London-based Simon Moore.

Moore, understandably, didn't like the idea. But then Sharon Stone informed him, 'Sam Raimi is the only person on my list and if Sam doesn't make the movie I don't think I will.' It went ahead.

Sharon Stone says of that time, 'I was adamant about Sam making this movie. I got to the point in the production that I was fighting for everything. People said I was a pain in the neck but that was OK, so having a reputation as a bitch makes people stay back a little bit. I don't mind it that much.'

But she needed another approach to seduce Leonardo DiCaprio to play The Kid, the Oedipal

☆ Is that a gun or are you just glad to see me? Leo gives co-star Sharon Stone the look.

gunslinger who duels with his father, played by Gene Hackman, who was himself hot from his Best Supporting Actor Oscar for *Unforgiven*.

DiCaprio was basking in the glory of *Gilbert Grape* and found the prospect of a big, mainstream commercial movie daunting. Sam Raimi wanted him badly for *The Quick and the Dead* explaining, 'Leo embodies the spirit of youth'. Sharon Stone was more colourful, 'He's so good, it's scary. I was dying to have him be in this movie. I would have carried the boy on my back to the set every day if that's what it would have taken.

'Luckily, Leonardo is down to earth and walked by himself.'

Only just.

'With *The Quick and the Dead* I really had to think about it for a long time. It was not my idea of the type of movie I wanted to do next. I turned it down ten to twenty times, so often I can't remember. Then on the last day they said: "Hey, we really want you and this is the last day you can have this role because we are going to hire somebody else." Everyone around me was saying: "Look, this is a good movie."

'I had this thing about not doing big commercial movies because most of the mainstream movies are just pieces of garbage that have been done thousands of times. But then I looked at *The Quick and the Dead* and I thought: "OK, Sharon Stone's in it and I think, disregarding her superstardom, the woman definitely has something going on. And Gene Hackman's in it and Sam Raimi is a completely innovative director. My character is somebody that's so completely insecure in himself that he has to put on a show to dazzle everybody and that to me started to become interesting.

'But The Kid was cool at the same time. He developed that thing about being cool. He wasn't afraid of anybody except for his father – and that was Gene Hackman. So I thought: "Look, I'm not working. I could do something different and I can have fun with this movie and why not?" So I did it.

'There's a difference between something that's mainstream and big budget and schlocky and doing

something that's mainstream and big budget and has something interesting in it. I just went there and did what I had to do and it was fun and I'm glad I did it.'

With Sharon Stone – who famously forgot to wear her knickers in the police interrogation scene in *Basic Instinct* – intimately involved, much was made of her romantic interlude with DiCaprio in *The Quick and the Dead*.

And The Kiss.

Stone, the ultimate screen sex symbol for the first half of the 1990s, gave this review: 'I looked at Leo and I thought: "I must have kissed boys when I was nineteen. But now they are forty-year-olds." So this was in a way the first time I'd ever kissed a nineteen-year-old. It was a lot like kissing your arm.'

DiCaprio was disappointed. And not impressed. In fact, his reaction was stone cold: 'I was expecting a little more from ol' Sharon, you know? I wasn't going to get down and dirty with her but it was sort of a letdown.'

The romance scene – the sex is not seen but they wake up together – was arguably a tactical error on Stone's part as producer and leading lady. When she and DiCaprio are seen in bed together she has a cruel hangover and he is saying he won her in a poker game. The questionable plot motivation of the circumstances did not concern Janet Maslin the perceptive film critic of the *New York Times* who wrote: 'Commanding enough limelight to show why the camera loves him, [Leonardo DiCaprio] is immensely promising. And a brash, scrawny adolescent who is nicknamed "The Kid" can make even the most glamorous movie queen look like his mother.'

But overall DiCaprio found his co-star 'not a bag of snot – very down to earth.' The critics, though dismissive of Stone, found him a winner. 'DiCaprio is well on his way to the held-back cockiness of the young Jack Nicholson, and it's hard to see how he can veer away from stardom now,' said Anthony Lane in *The New Yorker*.

And he enjoyed himself. The gunplay, like the swordplay in *The Man in the Iron Mask*, took him back to even younger days. 'I was called The Kid but I wasn't

I wasn't going to get down and dirty with her but it was sort of a letdown.

☆ Posing Boy: doing the 8 x 10 part for the publicity machine.

☆ **With the cast of** *The Quick and the Dead*, **Sharon Stone, Gene Hackman and Russell Crowe.**

Billy the Kid, I was a completely different character. I was fast. I was cool. I was into guns.

'I *had* to be very cool with the antique Colts I used in the film. It was very, very bad if I dropped one of them.'

Arizona was a lonely place for him. He was the only youngster on the set in Mescal – but not the only acting fledgling. He was a veteran compared to Sharon Stone's brother Michael who would later date Madonna and who offered DiCaprio yet another view of the dark side of Hollywood.

Michael Stone isn't a pretty picture like his sister. His nose has been broken several times and he spent two years in New York's Attica prison for possessing a kilo of cocaine. Stone, who was 45 in 1997, explained, 'I was a marijuana smuggler in the 1970s and then just got swept into the major league. With me, smoking a joint was small in comparison to being totally whacked out of your mind on alcohol. I was in the Air Force after graduating from school, and after I got out I began dealing drugs. I guess I was trying to buy my way out of the working class. I resented the fact that my father spent his whole life working in the steel shop. I thought that I could beat the system.

'Had it not been for Sharon and my parents I probably would still be in jail.'

He had been studying acting. Sharon Stone suggested him for *The Quick and the Dead*. She laughs: 'They were like: "OK, we've got to see her brother." But they kept putting it off until the bigger parts were cast and we had Gene Hackman and Leo and then my brother came in and they said: "Oh, he's fabulous!" I was so happy about it. He's a good, natural actor.'

Michael Stone did not have one line to say in the film. But DiCaprio was impressed. 'He was a good guy. And it was an example of family and I'm all for that. I think we *all* should be helping each other.'

Even now DiCaprio was not familiar to mass cinema audiences. But by contrast he was a regular in teen magazines. If he was avoiding being 'hunk of the week'

☆ **The head-to-toe crumpled look.**

☆ **Nose to nose with Oscar maverick Gene Hackman.**

on screen, he was being paraded as such in print. He was also flirting with the girls, and the gossip columns continued to label him 'the new James Dean' or – something that he found annoying and unsettling – as 'the replacement River Phoenix'.

His view of romance at this time was not romantic: 'I'll date anyone I can get along with. Anyone who has "a certain something" is OK with me.'

When did he lose his virginity? 'I don't want to talk about that.' But it happened somewhere between eighth grade in Hollywood and ... well, 28 May 1997, when he was leaving the Bowery Bar in New York.

He was about to put his anonymous date into a limousine when he saw Russian emigré model Galina with whom he'd been exchanging smiles and glances all evening. He offered her a lift, found the other girl a taxi, and took off to his uptown Manhattan hotel. Galina reported: 'He was not very romantic – not even thank you, ma'am.'

His list of dates is endless. He says Juliette Lewis who worked with him in *Gilbert Grape* is just 'a great pal' but others insist it was his first 'serious' romance. He met Sara Gilbert, the TV daughter on *Roseanne*, when they were both teenage TV actors and they've enjoyed what is described a 'buddy romance'. DiCaprio has also done some turkey trotting with teenage model Bijoux Phillips, the daughter of John 'Mamas and the Papas' Phillips, stepsister of actress-singer Chynna Phillips.

In New York the two all but took over the Lucky Strike bar in SoHo and went wild – with chewing gum. They had a dozen different varieties stuck to their table. Then they ordered turkey with stuffing, something not on the menu. Then, as he and Bijoux were partying at The

☆ 'The new 'James Dean' or 'the replacement River Phoenix'?

☆ Quick on the draw: Leo aiming to be the fastest gun alive.

The first kiss I had? It was the most disgusting thing in my life!

Flamingo on New York's West 21st Street, he found things getting too hot with the model, and so the staff very obligingly smuggled him out of the back door.

But DiCaprio wasn't so restrained in SoHo's chic Casa La Feme restaurant at the 'Look of the Year' contest – the American final of the Élite Modelling Agency's talent competition. As well as the ten finalists, there were dozens of John Casablanca's models around the place.

'He was running around wild, like a kid in a candy store,' said one of the organizers.

And, of course, in a way that's what he was.

'He was hopping from seat to seat, table to table, trying to court as many of the girls as he could. The girls were thrilled – Leonardo was one of the few cute guys out there and a star to boot. The rest of the men were your typical older lecher types.'

Young Romeo DiCaprio had eyes only for Rene Wiebensohn, a young model from a small Iowa town. 'Rene's a stunning all-American girl with sandy blonde hair and stands about 5ft 11ins', said Elite's Elizabeth Gabbay. Apparently DiCaprio later turned up at the Shoreham Hotel where the model girls were staying, chaperoned by Miss World contestants. DiCaprio tried to find his way in to see Rene Wiebensohn but according to Elizabeth Gabbay, 'To the best of my knowledge Leonardo didn't make it as far as Rene's room. Certainly there was no misconduct of any sort.'

He tells a similar story about his first ever date.

'I saw Meg Ryan and Billy Crystal in *When Harry Met Sally...* when I was on my first date. I went with this girl named Cessi, this beautiful little Spanish girl. I was in the eighth grade.

'We had this beautiful relationship over the phone all summer she was away and we were so close and so bonded and we'd tell each other everything. And then she came home and we went to the movies for the first time and, oh God, I wanted it to be so perfect.

'So I put on my light blue turtleneck, which I thought was cool at the time. It was a turtleneck I bought at K-mart [a Woolworth-style supermarket] or something. When I saw Cessi I was petrified and I couldn't even look her in the eye or speak to her. This was after telling her my deepest thoughts throughout the summer – that's the way humans are. And then we saw *When Harry Met Sally...* and I couldn't move, I couldn't look at her in the seat or anything.

'But the movie took me away. For two hours I was at peace because she was watching the movie and I didn't have this responsibility on me to be 'Superboy'. And then afterwards I remember eating a French dip and I was trying to get some control of the situation. So I was trying not to put her down exactly, but I was looking at her like she was ridiculous or something while she was eating this French dip. And she was really shy. And finally she said: "Do you have a problem with me eating this sandwich?" And I said: "No, not, not at all." But I was acting really weird.

'And that was our last date. I was in love with her for a year after that but I couldn't go near her because I was so mortified.'

DiCaprio starts getting candid.

'The first kiss I had? It was the most disgusting thing in my life! The girl injected about a pound of saliva into my mouth and when I walked away I had to spit it all out. It was awful.

'It's pretty disgusting when you think about it. I mean, people are concerned about eating off the same fork as someone else and – even though they like somebody – do you know that the human mouth is one of the dirtiest things on this planet? Even, a dog's mouth is cleaner. There's so much bacteria and disgusting slime and trapped food and bad breath in a mouth ...' He pulls himself up with an embarrassed look. 'I'm just saying, I'm just explaining ...'

If that weren't enough, there were the boys to kiss. Men including British actor David Thewlis.

SHOOTING STAR

"THE ONLY UNREADABLE
THING IS THAT NOTHING
IS UNREADABLE."
NINETEENTH CENTURY FRENCH POET
ARTHUR RIMBAUD

By the mid-1990s it seemed that Leonardo DiCaprio was a back page gossip column accident just temporarily parked before making the front page. There appeared to be incredible rage at his youth and talent – he wanted to make good movies, he wanted to have a good time. He liked girls. Gosh, he even liked his parents. It was all a runaround mix for the media. But the more that was made of his foibles – here was a young man who liked young girls – the more he seemed to just get on with his life *his* way.

Still he kept getting into corners over the River Phoenix tragedy. This was compounded by his decision in the early part of 1994 to play the poet and musician Jim Carroll in the film *Basketball Diaries*. Carroll was a 1970s hustler and heroin addict whose 1978 *Basketball Diaries* biography – somewhere between Salinger's *Catcher in the Rye* and the drug-influenced work of William Burroughs – had often been studied by Hollywood producers.

Carroll's themes of basketball, poetry and heroin meant that once again DiCaprio was linked with the drug issue. But it was something the young star felt intent on dispelling. 'With River it was sad but it is really ridiculous

to experiment with drugs for a movie. For a couple of months of work you're going to experiment with heroin and get hooked for life? The talk still goes on that I'm the "new" River Phoenix and all the drug stuff got beaten up while I was filming *Basketball Diaries* in New York.

'They were suggesting that I was in trouble which was total bullshit. I'd always liked River's work – I'm discounting the drugs and whatever he did in his personal life because the drugs weren't who he was. But as far as his acting and as far as who he was as a person, I respected him a lot.

'I think I'm different from him but I hope that I can somehow be thought of as someone who is unique and thoughtful, someone whose work will be respected. That is why you make films like *Basketball Diaries*. The Jim Carroll story was not just about drugs for me. For a person of my age then it was one of the best stories around.'

The story is based on the Manhattan adolescence of Carroll, a basketball player of class – a 'hoopster' – and at the same time a poet and junkie. He shot basketballs and heroin. It's about a New York Catholic high school basketball team who, in the movie, are also a bunch of swaggering sociopaths. DiCaprio as Carroll stands apart

☆ **Keeping the diary on sport and drugs.**

☆ (Above and right) Times get loud and wild in the *Basketball Diaries*.

because of his poetry – he has an artificial, almost golden, *glow*. An airball, you might say. He also turns gay tricks to pay for his drugs. The book includes graphic descriptions of homosexual hustling and SM sex.

The film is set in the 1970s but it was felt the story had a new relevance in the 'heroin chic' 1990s. The director, rock-video veteran Scott Kalvert, turned Carroll's elegiac look at life on the streets into his vision of almost everyday challenges for the post Just-Say-No generation.

For a new generation dealing with renewed pressures, DiCaprio's performance as Jim Carroll is a triumph. Co-starring as his best friend and fellow junkie was 'Marky' Mark Wahlberg, the naughty but muscled Calvin Klein underwear model. Harvey Keitel's former wife Lorraine Bracco, the straight-talking star of movies such as *GoodFellas*, played DiCaprio's mother. Her critical opinion of DiCaprio's talents is characteristically direct, 'The kid's a great fucking actor, OK?'

What's more he began to be involved in the film-making decisions. To date, this was the project he cared most about. 'The *Basketball Diaries* was the first time

He didn't have all that Hollywood director shit going on.

where I actually read a script and didn't want to put it down.

'I met Scott Kalvert the director, who hadn't done a movie before. He had done those Marky Mark videos so I thought that might be a bit of a problem. I wanted to do this movie but I didn't want it to turn out to be some "After School Special" about drugs, which is how it could have been. But when I met Scott he seemed like a cool guy. He didn't have all that Hollywood director shit going on.

'And he was willing to listen to my opinions.'

Inevitably this new status led to clashes with the director. DiCaprio goes on, 'I'll tell you this story: we were looking for someone to play this kid Mickey, and Scott wanted to bring in Marky Mark. He'd worked with him and really liked him. And like any normal human being I freaked out!

'I figured someone who is a singer – of, what's more, music I don't particularly like – was not right for the part. I told Scott we couldn't audition him. He said: "I worked with Marky and you gotta stop thinking that he's gonna pull some macho thing with the film. He's not like that. When you get to know him he's a really cool guy."

'And I said: "No. No. No. Absolutely NO."

'I told Scott that there were plenty of cool people out there – just find one of them. But then finally I thought about it and said: "Look I know if I had done something like Marky Mark did, and had a bad reputation, I'd feel really bad if some young actor wrote me off because he was in some good place in his career."

'We read so many kids for the character but everyone just didn't get it. And so I met Marky and as soon as I met him I wanted to find something wrong with him because I had this fear of what other people were gonna think of him and what I'm gonna think of him, like he's gonna do something terrible in the movie.

Scandal sells... I want to hear about Joe Blow the actor doing drugs...

'But as soon as he came in he was really cool and he said hello so matter-of-factly and did the scene and I couldn't help but be charmed by what he did. He brought an element of reality to it – he brought an element of being *really* street, because that's what he is. And he was the best person for the role by far. But I still had this problem. I didn't want to admit it. And finally I got myself to say: "OK, he's the best person for the role. I can't see anyone doing it much better than him. He's Marky Mark, so what? We'll do it."

'I got a lot of shit from people about him being in the film but, hey, it's what you do. He was great in the role. He was hot shit.'

Which is how he might have described some of the stories that were swirling around Manhattan during the filming. The *New York Post* wrote: 'DiCaprio hits Manhattan clubs and brawls with locals.' And: 'Juliette Lewis and Leonardo DiCaprio – two lovebirds who seldom rest in the nest – were all over each other at Rouge the other night.'

He says that he found the stories difficult to accept given that he was putting in fifteen-hour days on the movie. But he does understand celebrity: 'Scandal sells. Come on, I'll admit it. I want to hear about Joe Blow the actor doing drugs on the corner, that's interesting to me. You know, I'm like everybody else: "I really respect his work but did you know he's doing heroin? Oh, God, that's terrible, tell me more about it." So these columnists make it sound like I go to clubs, wreck myself silly, get into fights and sleep with all the ratty girls there.

'It's true that while we were filming, Marky and I went out for a little dancing, a little socializing, a little flirting. And one morning we wake up to find that according to the paper I picked a fight with Derrick Coleman the basketball player who's a forward for the New Jersey Mets. Like I'm going to get into an argument with him. Yo, Derrick. He's six-foot a hundred, seven-foot tall. He could spill a drink on me and I wouldn't fight!

'Supposedly, I got into a fight with him and Marky comes to save the day and help defend me. I could just

☆ Suits you sir – boys night out.

see my skinny white self fighting with the guy. So they wrote up a lot of garbage about us which is cool, I guess. What the hell ...'

Some of the stories, suggesting a link between the *Basketball Diaries'* subject matter and DiCaprio's own behaviour, were less funny. 'I'm doing a film that deals with this kid who has nothing going wrong for him but gets trapped in this world of drugs. And his whole life completely changes. He pushes off everything in his life just for this heroin addiction. And I don't do drugs!

'I don't do drugs and I've never done drugs in my life. I'm just not interested. If my friends start doing drugs they're going to hear about it from me. What people don't realize is that half the reason I did the *Basketball Diaries* is because of the whole heroin craze. I wasn't using heroin and I wasn't getting into brawls. On the set for the drugs scenes I snorted Ovaltine. At the end of every day I had to use a Q-Tip to scrape the chocolate powder from inside my nose. I'm not saying I was doing a "Say No To Drugs" special or anything, but I wanted to

☆ **Getting a talking to in** *Basketball Diaries.*

help, make some kind of statement against heroin. But then, of course, people decide I'm into it, right?

'There is no winning – look at the stories about me. Marky and I would go out. New York, it's a fucking hard town. We had a good time at clubs at weekends but that was all – it was escalated into something different.

'People want you to be a crazy, out-of-control brat. They want you miserable – just like them. They don't want heroes. People want companionship in their victim-ization – that's the burden. I can relate to that need but I'm not going to feed it. What they want is to see you fall – "you're no better than me! You're just like us!" '

Despite the press, DiCaprio maintains a calm and professional attitude to his public. 'I'm pretty happy-go-lucky,' he says. 'I hear of a lot of people having a problem with people approaching them, wanting to take pictures and meet them and get an autograph and whatnot. I've never really minded it. Unless somebody is going to be violent towards me, the worst that's going to happen is that somebody is going to want an autograph or to shake your hand or talk to you for a couple of seconds, and that's never harmed anyone. I have no problem with that. There's some odd situations sometimes that everybody sort of endures, but that's just like life. It's a small price to pay, I think, for the kind of work I get to do.'

The price includes, of course, constant media surveillance. 'I'm a guy who goes out with his friends. My mistake sometimes is that I think I can actually be like a normal human being and have fun and go to normal places. I'm realizing that I have to watch out for *everything* I do. I certainly don't think I'm

leading a destructive life – at least compared to other people my age.

'I just try to loosen up after work. I don't want to sit in a hotel room to avoid people who are writing things about me, eighty percent of which aren't true. People keep saying: "Don't you care about all of this?" But I don't. I really don't.

'I really like to have sweet people around me. I can't stand bad-asses. There's too many of them, especially my age, in Los Angeles. I like to get to know people and with these people you have to peel away so many layers. Just give me someone who's relaxed and cool to hang out with even if they're not studs. I have a good group of friends, people I've accumulated over the years. The main thing for me is just to maintain my life with my family and friends – they treat me like Leo, not like "Leonardo Master Thespian". That's all I need to maintain my sanity. Some I've known since elementary school, some I've met recently.

I don't do drugs and I've never done drugs in my life. I'm just not interested.

☆ Leo and *Basketball Diaries* co-star Matt Walhberg, who himself became a major Hollywood player in 1998 with *Boogie Nights*.

☆ On court and taking a dive.

'They're just a great crowd of guys and gals and I think they like me too – though you're never sure. No, I know they like me. It's not really about that. Our friend-ships are completely separate from everything else. I hardly know anybody who's in showbusiness. It seems like I do from all the writing about me but I really don't.' Nevertheless friends include Johnny Depp, Stephen Dorff, Christina Ricci, Juliette Lewis, Nicolas Cage's former long-time girlfriend Kristin Zang, Alicia 'Batgirl' Silverstone, Britain's Kate Winslett, Gaby Hoffman and Mark Wahlberg.

Naturally, he also finds himself surrounded by agents, managers and other Hollywood professionals. It is his father, though, whose opinion he most respects. 'It's my father who has lot to do with choosing films. He and I both read the scripts and he gives his opinion and I give mine. My father and I agree almost all the time. We haven't disagreed yet.'

They both loved the concept of a major movie about nineteenth-century French poet Arthur Rimbaud, the Liam Gallagher of his day, a teenage *enfant terrible* (he abandoned poetry at age 20) who was rude, mad and bisexual. 'In France,' said DiCaprio, 'Rimbaud is like James Dean.'

British playwright Christopher Hampton, (*Carrington*, *Dangerous Liaisons*) had studied Rimbaud's work at Oxford and adapted the film from one of his early plays. *Total Eclipse* (the title an unfortunate hint as to its box-office performance) was directed by Agnieszka Holland, previously Oscar-nominated for *Europa, Europa*, who personally picked DiCaprio for her hero following the death of first choice River Phoenix. Hampton, fifty-two in 1998, who had had four original plays successfully staged at the Royal Court Theatre in London before he was aged twenty-five, would later call Holland's direction 'too confrontational'.

Rimbaud's outrageousness – fuelled by hashish washed down with much absinthe – was reflected in his work and also in his relationship with established but

☆ A troubled life goes into the diary.

☆ **On the Basketball buses.**

'outsider' poet Paul Verlaine, played by the raging David Thewlis. The British actor, himself an award winner for *Naked*, found it 'a joy' working with DiCaprio.

Director 'Agnie' Holland was complementary as well: 'He was willing to take chances and you have to challenge yourself and the audience. Otherwise, what's the point? Leo was always willing to go for it.'

She was aware of the bad boy comparisons being made during the shooting of the film between DiCaprio, his character and also River Phoenix: 'Look, Leo is the best actor of his generation but it's sadistic building someone up and then waiting for them to fall. I was with River Phoenix for a couple of months before he died and I see him as a victim of this attitude. It's awful, just awful.'

So was Rimbaud's behaviour. He lived in a time before rock stars but nevertheless had a rock star attitude and his writing remains admired by artists like Bob Dylan and Patti Smith. That other bad boy legend, the late Jim Morrison, was also a fan. For DiCaprio this was part of the attraction. 'I wanted to do the part because Rimbaud was such a badass. But he was a genius so he had the goods to back it up. I think the people who liked the movie liked Rimbaud. We made it in France and he is still a god there.' He shrugs off the film's detractors, 'I think people expect me to go a certain way with my career

He was willing to take chances and you have to challenge yourself and the audience.

and that's not going to happen. I didn't do the next John Grisham movie and that troubled people.'

What did concern the young star was his on-screen love scenes with Thewlis – especially 'The Kiss'. He had just made the *Basketball Diaries* and it seemed he was getting a reputation for portraying characters with what someone described as 'slippery sexuality.' He was wary about it: 'I'm not a spokesperson on any of it, really, and not a practising ... I'm not part of that. It just seems to come up in films I'm interested in. I want to do some pretty crazy stuff – play a lizard man. I like what Gary Oldman did in *True Romance* – that kind of stuff.'

But he wants to make his thoughts clear: 'I don't have a problem doing a film about a relationship of love with another man. That's just acting, know what I mean? But as far as the kissing stuff goes that's really hard for me.'

On set before the scene was filmed he confided, 'I've faced the fact that I'm gonna have to do it and I'm gonna do it because I supposedly love the guy. I've never kissed a guy but when I do that scene I'm going to go in there and I'm going to walk over to him and I'm going to stick my tongue down his fucking throat and probably swerve it around a little bit.

'That's it. End of story. I will have no qualms about it. Some actors get drunk before they do scenes that scare them and that has to do with insecurity. If I commit myself to a movie I'm going to have go through with it. I think that's kinda cool.'

After the filming he said, 'I won't lie to you. Staging those scenes was uncomfortable

I won't lie to you. Staging those scenes was an uncomfortable situation to be in.

for me. Thankfully, David made things go as well as they possibly could.

'I don't worry that it might upset my fans. You can't decide on roles for that reason. If it's a great part – and this was for me – you have to go for it. Very little out there gets me excited. Usually I look at a script and go: "Can this possibly be more cliche-ridden?" *Total Eclipse* was risky but there should be more movies like it. It was a real, intelligent film.'

And he supported it – all the way to the National Arts Club in New York's Gramercy Park. Older members who had just heard a lecture on Buster Keaton were leaving as DiCaprio's fan club arrived for a party celebrating *Total Eclipse*. They were in a lively mood – displaying an attitude similar to Rimbaud's when he showed his disdain for the bourgeois poets by peeing on a group of them.

DiCaprio's brat pack were smoking rather than urinating. As they smoked pot in the Club's panelled ballroom one elderly female member asked a dreadlocked actor to put out his cigarette. She was told to 'Fuck off.' A guard was called and a guest reported: 'Next thing you know, fists were flying. The kids were fighting with the guards. A woman bartender jumped over the bar to get away. People were running to get their coats.'

Police were called to the party but DiCaprio and his guests, including actresses Cameron Diaz and Julia Ormond, had fled before they arrived. Director Agnieszka stayed, true to herself – and her movie.

'It was thrilling. It was life imitating art,' she said.

☆ All the troubles of the world on his young shoulders.

RAP ROMEO

"HE IS THE NEXT JAMES DEAN"
CLAIRE DANES ON DiCAPRIO
AUGUST 1996

Leonardo DiCaprio and William Shakespeare may not have seemed to have had much in common in 1996, but both had Web sites on the Internet and millions of teenage consumers. And movie deals.

The character of Hamlet had been seen on screen portrayed by Olivier, of course, Mel Gibson and even by Arnold Schwarzenegger (in a movie within a movie, *The Last Action Hero*) before Kenneth Branagh, in the title role, introduced America to his four-hour-long film version on Christmas Day 1996. Also playing globally at that time were Al Pacino's *Looking for Richard* and Sir Ian McKellen's *Richard III*, set in an alternative 1930s Britain. Former Royal Shakespeare Company director Trevor Nunn was also offering a conventionally handsome *Twelfth Night*.

So Shakespeare was a little ahead on done deals over DiCaprio, who had been agonizing about becoming James Dean for a bio-picture of the tragic star. He had been approached to headline the big budget film and Michael Mann, of *Miami Vice*, *The Last of the Mohicans* and *Heat* fame, was to direct. Then Mann bowed out. He was replaced by Des McAnuff who had guided *Tommy* on Broadway but he also left the proposed project. It was in limbo.

So was a movie by *Godfather* director Francis Ford Coppola, who wanted DiCaprio to play 'beat' generation writer Jack Kerouac in a screen version of Kerouac's book *On the Road*. Leonardo was, said all involved in the various projects, 'fabulously cool'. At the same time DiCaprio was most interested in appearing with Richard Gere in *Primal Fear* playing a stuttering choirboy accused of killing his bishop. Ironically, the broken-down negotiations with him led to a chance for another actor, Edward Norton. At the 1997 Oscars, Norton was a Best Supporting Actor nominee, losing out in the end to the pneumatic Cuba Gooding Jr. for *Jerry Maguire*.

It was the first screen role for Norton, then 27, an off-off-Broadway actor. A further irony for DiCaprio was that it was Shakespeare that got Norton into acting. As a teenager he saw Sir Ian McKellen in a one-man production titled *Acting Shakespeare* and he recalls: 'That's when it hit me on an adult level that acting could be something phenomenal.'

Norton, a classically trained actor, was superb in *Primal Fear*. But in the meantime DiCaprio whose theatrical education comprised 'ten pages of some Russian book with drama masks on the cover' had turned into a phenomenon.

His Shakespeare education was, he admits, a little lacking when Australian Baz Luhrmann approached him about the co-starring role in the movie to be officially titled *William Shakespeare's Romeo and Juliet*. Luhrmann, who had won international attention for his marvellous camp-cult, fun dance movie *Strictly*

☆ **Romeo as Beau Brummel, the velvet dandy look for Leo.**

Ballroom, wanted to turn the Bard's story into something for the vibrant, sexy 1990s, believing he could bring in young audiences. He saw the film as 'the story of two kids whose love is a rebellion against all the hatred surrounding them.'

As it turned out it was a kiss-kiss, bang-bang, way-out-there highly-stylised Shakespeare, which was to be termed 'ultra hip' and 'cool'. And that was just the highbrow critics. Luhrmann's *Romeo and Juliet* won an eclectic fan base, and a genuinely mass audience.

Shakespeare's words are kept, but spoken in a modern world where the Montagues and Capulets are battling corporations as well as families. With Mexico City – known as the 'millennial urban nightmare' – as the location, the citizens and their guns and cars and clothes are all flash, the landscape a cacophony of startling pinks, oranges and blues. Mercutio (played by Harold Perrineau) is a black drag queen; the Montagues are white and the Capulets are Hispanic, with echoes of *West Side Story.* Luhrmann wanted DiCaprio as Romeo from the outset but his would-be star was apprehensive: 'At first, I wasn't sure about doing it. I didn't want to run about in tights swinging a sword around. But Baz convinced me to go to Australia and meet with him for a week, and while I was there he figured out what his vision was and then I was really interested.'

Luhrmann's vision was of a wild-in-the-streets version of the classic romance. Verona was now Verona Beach and the action, the feuding, was alternatively set in the past, present and future. MTV newsreels and screaming tabloid headlines explained the story of the tragic lovers who are members of two feuding families. The opening scene has a television newscaster reading Shakespeare's prologue. DiCaprio loved it and took the plunge. 'If it hadn't been for Baz, I would have been really paranoid about doing the role, thinking about all the past Romeos

I didn't want to run about in tights swinging a sword around.

☆ Claire Danes on Leo: 'I still can't figure out whether he's really transparent or incredibly complex. I think he's the latter, but I don't know.'

In our version the ball takes place at a club and everybody's on drugs and dancing.

and how I would compare with them and whatnot. But when we first met he simply stated to me that we weren't doing a normal *Romeo and Juliet*. It was going to be different in every way and he even wanted to bring out my

and sort of scream it at times and try and bring it out so it was clear in our minds all the time what we were saying.'

'Those rehearsals contained very sweet moments,' remembers Luhrmann. 'We had fun trying to understand the text. One of the things we set out to do was to get them to claim the language for themselves, to make the words their own.'

Americanisms in all the Shakespeare. He wanted me to be really comfortable with the language and make it sound almost conversational instead of affected – like the English Shakespearean way, you know?

'As soon as I knew that I could sort of do it how I was, I became really comfortable. The only thing I objected to was Baz and the rollerblades. He wanted everybody on rollerblades at the beginning of the film: I couldn't see myself spouting Shakespeare on skates. The rest just sort of happened. He blocked out each of the verses for us. He took each line and dissected it and talked to us about what it meant, and we did exercises where we had to, like, feel the emotion for each word

For DiCaprio, then, it became his sort of Shakespeare. 'It meant that our *Romeo and Juliet* was a little more hard-core and a lot cooler than any other. Some people said, "You shouldn't mess with Shakespeare, you can't do that ..." But Shakespeare was a genius. I'm sure if he were alive he would have been totally behind Baz and what he was trying to do.

'He made it definitely surreal. At the ball where Romeo meets Juliet, Romeo's on drugs and you see him tripping out on Mercutio who is that black drag queen in the white Afro. Mercutio's wearing an Afro as part of his costume but I trip out on him and it grows about three feet. That's a wild scene.

☆ The fatal kiss of Romeo and Juliet.

'In our version the ball takes place at a club and everybody's on drugs and dancing. It's crazy. But the movie's very real too, and very different. As I said, I wouldn't have done it if I'd had to jump around in tights. If you never read *Romeo and Juliet*, it's like this classic story, blah, blah ... But if you really study it you see Romeo was, like, a gigolo who falls for this girl Juliet who says: "Look, if you've got the balls, put 'em on the table."

'It's about these things that carry you in a certain direction and you can't stop – like when people run off to Las Vegas to get married.

'That's the beauty of it.

'They both were people who had guts.'

The film meant several months of intense work on location in Mexico City, one of the poorest, most polluted capitals in the world. Everyone needed a lot of balls, or *cajones*, as the Mexicans have it, including Claire Danes, who was Luhrmann's Juliet. And DiCaprio's, but to how intimate a degree both have sworn never to reveal. They both say they had to 'bond' during the hazardous weeks of filming.

Claire Danes turned eighteen in April 1997 and like DiCaprio was a soaring star, thought of as one of Hollywood's most gifted young actresses. She was an Internet pin-up from her time in a cult television series, had rejected being in Steven Spielberg's *Schindler's List*, had lined up yet another adaptation of a John Grisham thriller – working for Francis Ford Coppola – and had a hat trick of films awaiting release. She was so busy she had to turn down the title role in a big budget *Joan of Arc*. She had also starred opposite Michelle Pfeiffer in *To Gillian on Her 37th Birthday*, sparking 1997 Oscar

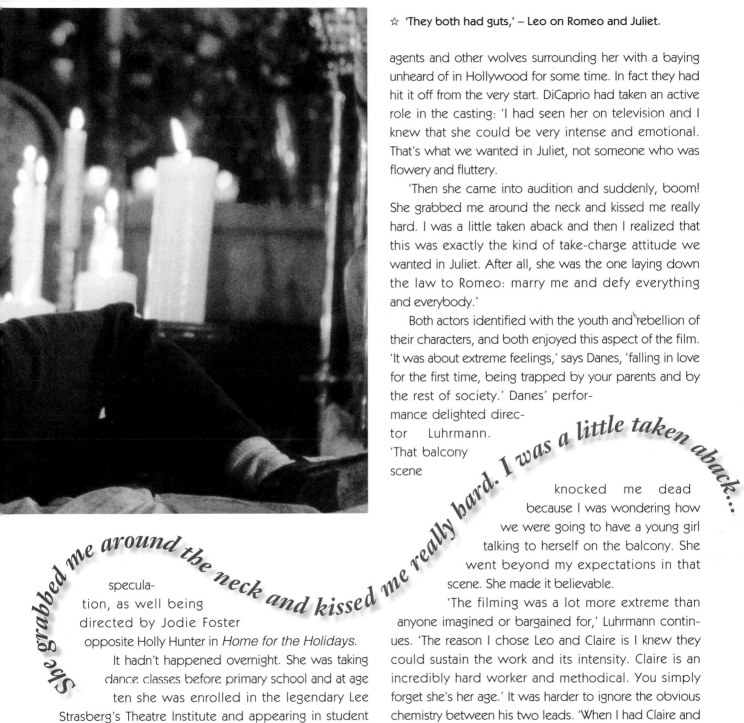

☆ 'They both had guts,' – Leo on Romeo and Juliet.

agents and other wolves surrounding her with a baying unheard of in Hollywood for some time. In fact they had hit it off from the very start. DiCaprio had taken an active role in the casting: 'I had seen her on television and I knew that she could be very intense and emotional. That's what we wanted in Juliet, not someone who was flowery and fluttery.

'Then she came into audition and suddenly, boom! She grabbed me around the neck and kissed me really hard. I was a little taken aback and then I realized that this was exactly the kind of take-charge attitude we wanted in Juliet. After all, she was the one laying down the law to Romeo: marry me and defy everything and everybody.'

Both actors identified with the youth and rebellion of their characters, and both enjoyed this aspect of the film. 'It was about extreme feelings,' says Danes, 'falling in love for the first time, being trapped by your parents and by the rest of society.' Danes' performance delighted director Luhrmann. 'That balcony scene knocked me dead because I was wondering how we were going to have a young girl talking to herself on the balcony. She went beyond my expectations in that scene. She made it believable.

'The filming was a lot more extreme than anyone imagined or bargained for,' Luhrmann continues. 'The reason I chose Leo and Claire is I knew they could sustain the work and its intensity. Claire is an incredibly hard worker and methodical. You simply forget she's her age.' It was harder to ignore the obvious chemistry between his two leads. 'When I had Claire and Leo – we called him "D" throughout the shoot – it was a moment-by-moment collaboration. They learned from each other and grew together.'

After filming Danes gave her co-star a gift of two chocolate eggs and a note saying: 'Don't say I never did anything for you, love Claire.'

She grabbed me around the neck and kissed me really hard. I was a little taken aback...

speculation, as well being directed by Jodie Foster opposite Holly Hunter in *Home for the Holidays*.

It hadn't happened overnight. She was taking dance classes before primary school and at age ten she was enrolled in the legendary Lee Strasberg's Theatre Institute and appearing in student films at New York and Columbia universities. For high school she went to a New York performing arts college.

Before working with DiCaprio she was seeing her Beverly Hills psychiatrist twice a week.

Nevertheless, DiCaprio could empathize with her; he could understand the pressure of the studios and talent

Despite the support of DiCaprio and her own enormous talent, she says she was terrified when it came to filming the immortal balcony scene: 'That was so intimidating to do. I mean, it was ridiculous to get so worked up about it but I did.

'I had to go on and say those famous lines that have been made fun of over the years. I had to throw away all these other perfor- mances and interpretations – just put them behind me and start from scratch.

'I had such a panic attack. I'd just seen the Olivia Hussey version [Franco Zeffirelli's 1968 film] and she was so gorgeous. So I had a little breakdown at three in the morning.

'I'm self-conscious about my looks; I'm not secure in that area. It's, like, amazing how frightening that is.

'It wasn't an easy movie. We were in Mexico for four months and I was the only girl. The testosterone was running wild and it seemed we were in a different world. The movie's also about gangs so there were a whole bunch of little boys running around causing havoc. It's a very different thing when you are just talking to them one-to-one. It was a lot of fart jokes and fooling around with the prosthetics from the make-up trailer; a lot of mooning. I was not really in my element.'

Mexico City offered a frightening view of street school – and DiCaprio and the boys at play.

It was, says DiCaprio, a 'wild' time. They suffered from Montezuma's Revenge, were sick with dysentery, and also had to cope with a film crew member being kidnapped and friends being beaten up.

On top of all that, with all the youngsters from Hollywood and New York on the Mexico City set there were *antics*. Paul Rudd who played Romeo's rival suitor, Paris, reported: 'I think it was a little more wild than it needed to be. DiCaprio's best friend walking around the hotel naked asking the security guards for a key to his room – and we were all sitting there filming it on video. It was insane.'

Sitting together during promotional work on the film DiCaprio and Danes had a frightening story to tell. They had gone out on a 'date' to a club in the city with one of DiCaprio's friends. Danes elaborates: 'Oh, man, that night at the nightclub was insane – that security guard just picked a fight with one of Leo's friends who was visiting from Los Angeles. My best friend from the set and I went inside and ...'

DiCaprio carries on the narrative: 'I went in after you, once I saw things heating up. When we got back my friend was messed up. His ribs were broken. It was a good

A lot of strange things happened that night...

☆ Stairway to decadence.

It must have been a full moon...

thing I was inside or I would have got all fucked up too. It's strange. I think some of that helped us. We were in a movie dealing with violence and suffering and guns and we were getting a real-life taste of it.

'I think if we had shot it in Los Angeles in a sort of relaxed atmosphere it would not have been the same movie. I think that all the sort of stuff we were hearing about every day, about the violence around, the chaos that was going on in Mexico City, fuelled all the guys and all the actors to really sort of ... We were all sort of crazed about what was going on. Some people from our hotel

getting killed – it, like, gave us some incentive in our parts.

'Every one of the actors got sick at one point or another. Baz got to the point where he had to have an IV of glucose in his arm he was so sick, so dehydrated. I got terribly sick and Claire got really sick so we all had a week off. We had to recuperate.'

'Everyone was getting stomped on for no reason', said Danes, adding quietly, 'That was the same night that guy got kidnapped.'

'A lot of strange things happened that night,' said DiCaprio intriguingly, before adding, 'It must have been a full moon ...'

YOUNG LOVE

"HE IS PARANOID THAT EVERYBODY THINKS HE'S GAY. HE IS NOT GAY"
CLAIRE DANES
AUGUST 1997

Full moon or not, the violence was certainly a distraction throughout the long weeks of filming. DiCaprio passed the time doing his classic Michael Jackson impersonations and taking off other cast members trying to deliver their Shakespeare impressively. 'I'd walk in front of the camera and Leonardo would do my line all screechy. "Thou or I must go!" ' recalls John Leguizamo, who played Tybalt in tight pants and a thin moustache, Cuban heels and a matador jacket. 'So the next time I'd become really self-conscious.' In mock horror he adds, 'I just hated him because it came so easy to that little blond, happy golden-boy motherfucker.'

'He'd smoke a cigarette, do some laps in the swimming pool, do Michael Jackson, go on the set, and there it was.'

Director Lasse Hallstrom who guided DiCaprio in *What's Eating Gilbert Grape* backs up that view. 'It comes very easy to him. My only theory is that he has a connection to the four-year-old inside.'

DiCaprio enjoyed what some saw as childish behaviour. Baz Luhrmann, himself a victim, was accepting of it: 'People say that Marlon Brando was a constant practical joker and with "D" you might see thirty characters come out of him in a day. A regular sport with him was to impersonate me in fairly cruel, uncompromising ways.

'But acting is playing, and all that fooling around kept him in a constant state of playing.'

It paid off. DiCaprio saw the story through the eyes of *his* audience: 'I talked to my friends about it and I really didn't realize until then how much of Baz's creativity is really attractive to people my age. All the wild costumes and the guns and the sort of mad violence that's going around in the movie made people want to see it, to experience it. I approve of whatever will get them into the theatres to see a classic play. Because I was like that too at first. I was like: "Shakespeare, pleeease! It's too complicated. What the hell is he saying? You're going to have to give me an outline to watch this, to watch a movie from Shakespeare."

'I had that attitude too, but people my age responded to the new look and were attracted by it. And to believe in love and be ready to give up everything for it, especially at that age, to be willing to risk your life for it, is the ultimate tragedy. That's why it's a masterpiece.'

His views were endorsed on the UK high streets where *Romeo and Juliet* became a youth phenomenon with young audiences re-enacting the feuds between the Montagues and the Capulets after screenings. 'We were all tipping each other off about the crowds and the antics', said John Hughes of the Phoenix Cinema in Oxford. 'The message was the same: "The Montagues and the Capulets are on the way." '

Baz Luhrmann's vision that he could make Shakespeare relevant to the lives of late 1990s youth – and that he

☆ Leo and Claire Danes talking about their movie love in *Romeo and Juliet*.

☆ Until death us do part ...

Baz Luhrmann also saw the attraction of his young star – at first hand. 'All the Mexican girls were going mad over him. They were hunting us down. We were trying to throw ourselves in their way hoping he would rub off on us.'

DiCaprio liked the attention. Claire Danes is coy about it. John Leguizamo worked closely with this screen Romeo and Juliet partnership and comments: 'I think they had crushes on each other but they kept it very professional. Nothing was ever done. And that's great because when you consummate an attraction you totally defuse the tension on the screen.'

Luhrmann adds: 'There were arguments. Sometimes they were like two kids on holiday and sometimes it was like you were dragging your children through a desert and they were starving and suffering. But because they were so young and in the middle of such extraordinary events, I think they came to rely on each other which was a great thing to behold. On screen they were great together. She was strong with Leonardo and was someone you could believe was discovering the overpowering force of the love drug for the first time.'

Claire Danes admits she had 'great chemistry' with her Romeo.

All the Mexican girls were going mad over him. They were hunting us down.

could, with all the gunplay, vanquish the cobwebs of snobbery – paid off. As with *Grease* and *The Rocky Horror Picture Show*, audience participation became part of the experience for rural Romeos. And it wasn't always classical, or Shakespearean, participation either. As Romeo was being cheered on, some sections of the audience would urge Juliet to 'get your tits out' during the balcony scene. Also, DiCaprio was often given advice about what he should be doing to Claire Danes – and vice versa – as they tumbled in the sheets. DiCaprio was regarded by many male members of the audience as a Jack-The-Lad sort of Romeo.

'We really clicked. It's great when you find someone who you understand. It's to do with me having a lot of male in me and he has a lot of female in him.

'He's paranoid now because everyone thinks he's gay. He's *not* gay. He's not gay.' Danes says that with some assured insistence.

'Did I fall in love with Leonardo? Leonardo and I really like each other, we really respect each other. We were telling such a intense story and bearing the weight of such a commercial film. It was a complicated friendship ... he also did cartwheels and hit people over the head with Twizzlers.

'But the movie has brought me a lot of attention. Fame is scarier now. And, you know, girls like me because I kissed Leonardo DiCaprio. All the youngsters, all the teenagers, like me because of that!'

☆ A pledge of undying love. Romeo and Juliet connect.

The critics also liked her. And they loved DiCaprio, especially *Sight and Sound* magazine. The critical bible of the film industry, it reported: 'DiCaprio is skinny and gangly, seemingly all arms and legs. His walk, somewhat pigeon-toed, makes him seem very vulnerable. This version of the film places more onus on Romeo than Juliet. He is the one who bears the brunt of feeling: it's his face in close-up most of the time indicating how he wants, longs, feels and sometimes, eyes hidden by tears, suffers. His performance is all raw emotion. When he hears of Juliet's death it's not just that the camera lifts up suddenly to crush him that expresses his grief, but the way he falls on his pigeon-toe heels [sic]. It's a superb performance.'

For DiCaprio the whole excitement around the film was an endorsement of his career choices, but the gossip columns back home over the border were making much of the 'antics'. He was not bothered: 'I won't stay cooped up in my hotel room. Most famous people aren't out except in, like, their little bullshit dive bars or whatever. I don't want to become a strange person.

'I don't want to give up the life I have. My career should adapt to me and if it doesn't ... Fame is like a VIP pass wherever you want to go. Sharon Stone gave me a good piece of advice: "When you're famous you gotta accept it as an advantage. It will only make you stronger."

'I would have a nervous breakdown if I had to go through a movie for three months and be that character on and off set. I know what I'm doing but when they say "Cut" I'm fine. I can joke around.

'I don't hide in a corner and yell at anyone who tries to speak to me. I am kind of happy-go-lucky. It's hard to find the stuff to work off, when I have to do emotional scenes. I sort of make stuff up in my head. I had to do it in *Romeo and Juliet* more than any movie.

'Usually there are just some scenes where you're sort of wrecked and crying but with this I was wrecked and crying in almost every scene, in a shambles. Baz would understand that before each of these things I'd have to have like twenty minutes alone in a corner. I sort of just visualized horrible things and tried to make myself feel horrible. I remember I made stuff up about my family dying and whatever was going on in my life. Anything horrible I could think of mainly has to do with one of my parents dying. That's the main thing that gets me going.

'But, hey, I haven't gone crazy yet. I really do think I'm pretty well balanced considering the position I'm in. I think it has to do with me not investing everything in my job. All these actors think that "the blood in their veins is fuelled by acting".' Another sharp impersonation pops out. 'I'm happier when I'm not working, hanging out with my friends, doing something I love.

☆ **Action like Shakespeare never expected.**

'Don't get me wrong. I really love acting. It's fucking cool. I love it when it's really about acting. I love it when you have to create stuff and collaborate with the director. You feel like what you are doing is not going to waste. It's in the archives. It's going to be there for years. Michael Caton-Jones taught me that.

'You really can't constantly think about that pressure while you're shooting because if you do, then it's just gonna make you a hundred times worse. But I do think about that stuff all the time. It's a hard position to be in. Just because you may have done a good performance once, doesn't mean you're always going to be good.

'That's why some of the greatest actors in the world have gone a little bit nuts. They're saying to themselves: "What happened? You used to love me." It's an easy trap to fall into but I can't say I've found the answer for it.

☆ Shoulder holster gunplay; Leo more Bogart than Romeo.

'You could find me in the loony bin in a couple of years. But I don't care what people say about me anymore because it gets to the point that when you're hot you're hot and when you're not you're not.'

But he cannot disguise all the doubts: 'You just get the feeling all the time that, like, you gotta have more. And no matter how good it is, it's never enough. It's weird but I think the public expects that from you.

'They want you to keep going, otherwise you could fade away ...'

For DiCaprio, for the moment, this doesn't look likely. Not with Robert De Niro calling again. And Diane Keaton on the line.

And Meryl Streep wanting to mother you.

Leonardo DiCaprio was about to give what the *New York Times*'s most eminent critic would call his most 'broodingly magnetic' performance.

But with DiCaprio there was no telling what could happen next. Martin Brown, the co-producer of *William Shakespeare's Romeo and Juliet*, said that at the film's Hollywood premiere there were gasps from the celebrity-packed audience when DiCaprio first appeared on screen. Initially, he was at a loss to describe the atmosphere, then he came up with:

'It was like Beatlemania.'

But, hey, I haven't gone crazy yet...

DICING WITH DISASTER

"HE'S ALWAYS COMPELLING, YOU CAN'T WATCH ANYTHING ELSE WHEN HE'S ACTING"

MERYL STREEP ON LEONARDO DiCAPRIO

'Clueless', laughs Leonardo DiCaprio when quizzed about his relationship with *Batgirl* pin-up Alicia Silverstone. The actress had been making comments about him that ended with: 'I don't even want to talk about that guy.'

DiCaprio smiles calmly. 'Alicia and I did our first movies at about the same time. We've known each other for years. We're not really good friends or anything but we know each other.'

This is diplomatic stuff. Silverstone dumped her boyfriend, Beverly Hills hairdresser Moize Charrough, for DiCaprio. In the environment of teen Beverly Hills it became the talk of the village that not only had she stopped going out with Charrough, she had even stopped letting him cut her long, luxurious locks.

'Moize was devastated', reported a friend of Silverstone's, adding, 'He went to France on business and by the time he came back Alicia was in love with Leo. I guess she was impressed with him. He didn't act like some tripped-out movie star – he's a natural. And he offered her respected advice on how to handle stardom and the Hollywood scene. They were kids in love –

they'd go out to eat at cafés and stuff themselves with burgers, Coca-Cola and fries. And sit and talk.'

By then, DiCaprio was the superstar of the Young Hollywood set. When he hosted a party at the Bar Marmount in West Hollywood there was almost a riot. More than five hundred people had to be turned away. Actress Parker Posey waited two hours to get in. Demi Moore didn't get past the door.

DiCaprio says he just remained 'cool'. On his relationship with Silverstone and her candid remarks, he sticks to the diplomatic line. 'I'm sure she was asked some question that she thought was ridiculous and just said: "I'm not even going to answer that question." Just like I would do.'

He is more forthcoming about two other ladies – Meryl Streep and Diane Keaton, with whom he starred in *Marvin's Room*. Not forgetting De Niro, to whom he says he will always be grateful for his first break. 'On *This Boy's Life* De Niro helped and I got the part. From that point on it's been pretty smooth. That got me *Gilbert Grape* and it was sort of my foot ... whatever you call it ... my foothold.'

☆ The woman millions hate: Leo's model girl Kristen Zane, the former lover of Oscar winner Nicolas Cage.

Marvin's Room further strengthened DiCaprio's reputation. De Niro produced as well as co-starred in the film, and in July 1997 found himself in Russia to accept the honours when the film won the Golden St George grand prize as Best Picture at the Moscow International Film Festival.

In the picture DiCaprio is the troubled oldest son of single mother Meryl Streep, living in Ohio. When she discovers her estranged sister Diane Keaton is suffering from leukaemia in Florida, she packs her teenagers into the car and heads off, starting the wheels on a black comedy focusing on family relationships and the meaning of love. It all revolves around Keaton's need for a bone marrow transplant, and because of it, her need to contact the sister she has not seen in twenty years. There follows a touching story about the need for laughter in the face of tragedy.

DiCaprio worked well with his Oscar-winning co-stars. As the resentful son Hank he played off Streep's wilful, selfish mother.

The family situation was so different from his own. 'I didn't have much to identify with. But acting with somebody like Meryl Streep keeps you on your toes. She does stuff out of left field sometimes. I mean, she'll do a scene the same way four times and then, all of a sudden, she'll have a new twist on a line. I learned a lot from her. She's a consummate actress.

☆ **Different shades of opinion: Diane Keaton and Leo.**

☆ **Diane Keaton and Meryl Streep.**

'She was completely unlike any other actress that I've ever worked with just because I'd never met anybody who could just sort of walk onto a set and sort of without saying anything just have complete and utter respect. You feel this energy when she walks in and everyone sort of becomes silent. And it's this thing she has when she acts. When I first started, when I did my first scene with her she was all over the place. I was thinking, "What's she doing?" It was so unlike anything I'd ever seen before. She did some wild things and then you see it on film and everything she does seems completely natural and real. It was a big shock for me to work with Meryl Streep because I had never worked with an actress like that.

'Claire Danes has a lot of the attributes; she's like Meryl in a way. She possesses a lot of power too, and the ability to get so into character.'

DiCaprio contrasts this with his own approach. 'I've never really been the

type of person to stay in character. If I were deeply into each of my characters I'd be in a mental ward. I'm fine because I figured out that you don't have to immerse yourself completely into a character in order to do a good job. I like to keep things light.' In this respect, he found a soul-mate in his other co-star in *Marvin's Room*. 'That was what was great about working with Diane Keaton. She has the best laugh in the world – and it's easy to make her laugh.'

He enjoyed a similarly relaxed relationship with English actress Kate Winslett, with whom he was to co-star in the most expensive film ever made – a movie that would open with

She has the best laugh in the world – and it's easy to make her laugh.

incredible fanfare across America in more than 2,500 cinemas.

The story has it that before disaster struck five days into its maiden voyage in April 1912, passengers on the $7.3 million *Titanic* went to bed expecting that the

I definitely wanted to try at least once in my career something of this incredible magnitude.

liner would dock on, or even ahead, of schedule. The film version by movie-mastermind James Cameron – whose blockbuster credits include *Aliens* and *Terminator 2*: and *True Lies* – didn't sink but rather sailed on and on and on ... the release delays costing, according to estimates, anywhere between $20 and $30 million.

Initially scheduled as a 1997 summer 'event' for America's 4 July weekend, the most technically ambitious film *ever* – costing more than $200 million – finally surfaced at the start of 1998. It had involved the building of a nearly life-size, five-story replica of the ocean liner and a tank big enough to hold it, and six months of filming and special effects creation using the dazzlingly realistic new digital technology. With so much involved, the delays were inevitable.

☆ 'This sounds like the biggest, naffest cliché but we were like brother and sister.' Kate Winslet on her 'romance' with Leo during the filming of *Titanic*.

Cameron, working seventeen hours a day, seven days a week, was at the centre of a film so vast – with a budget rivalling the financially disastrous 1963 Elizabeth Taylor/Richard Burton *Cleopatra* – that it could rewrite the future of film. Certainly, with so much invested in the budget by Paramount Studios ($65 million) and Rupert Murdoch's Fox Studios (the balance) many careers in management boardrooms and before and behind the cameras were at risk.

The question *Titanic* always posed was just *how big* can a Hollywood film get? And, also, would it sink or swim? And for the Hollywood optimists, how many

Oscar nominations? An early 'cut' of the film was described by many as a 'masterpiece'. Certainly, it was heralded as a moving, sweeping, passionate romantic drama on a grand scale. An epic of impressive high-technology proportions. This was hugely heartening for its young stars.

DiCaprio and Kate Winslett had found themselves at the centre of a landmark project, one often compared to legendary British film-maker David Lean's *Dr Zhivago*. The film's production crew numbered more than 800 people and they seemed to take over the location with their custom-built studio in Rosarito Beach, Mexico, a cheap weekend runaway-hideaway in Baja California.

'Oh, boy, this *Titanic* thing was just another ball game', said DiCaprio with his piano keyboard grin. 'I'd never done a movie like it. You arrive on the set and you see thousands of people who are involved with it – it's just such a gigantic thing. You've got to keep a sense of yourself and of your character at all times and not concentrate on the wild madness that's going on around you. It was a completely different experience. I definitely wanted to try at least once in my career something of this incredible magnitude.

'It wasn't really the story of the *Titanic* but the scale of the film which really got me. If I was going to do a big budget film this was going to be it. I didn't want to do a superhero movie or a monster movie or anything like that. I didn't want to be an action hero.

'I wanted to be a regular guy in a larger-scale picture, and this was the first one that had a real character in it – an interesting character – *and* a story. And then surrounded by the *Titanic*, which is, like, one of the biggest disasters; I know there have been other *Titanic* films but this is, like, James Cameron's *Titanic*, which is a whole other ballgame.'

Cameron, who has a reputation for detail and perfection, has also been criticized for being more involved in the technical rather than the human aspects of his films.

☆ 'He's probably the world's most beautiful looking man,' says *Titanic* co-star Kate Winslet.

DiCaprio didn't find that: 'He certainly doesn't ignore actors. That's for sure. I've always had a prejudice against big budget box office things like this, and I never really wanted to try it. But I looked at this script and I liked the whole story, the love story, and asked myself if I would do it if it wasn't going to cost millions and millions of dollars to shoot and I answered "Yes". I decided not to be prejudiced.

'James Cameron wrote this and he knows the whole movie relies on the love story between Kate Winslett and me. He gave us a lot of attention. I'm Jack, a young artist from Paris, and I've been working there and doing drawings and whatnot and she's Rose, an upper class girl – I'm third class. We start messing around. I meet her world and she meets mine.

'She's engaged to someone else and then for the second half of the film the ship starts to sink ... then everything is chaotic.'

Kate Winslett was already a fan of DiCaprio's before they met on the set of *Titanic*. In fact, she confesses that she had longed to play Juliet opposite DiCaprio, but adds: 'I knew I was too old. The casting of Claire Danes was brilliant. She's a wonderful actress.' Winslett hadn't let the grass grow under her feet, though. Only 22 in 1998, she had already starred in *Heavenly Creatures*, *Jude*, *Sense and Sensibility* and as Ophelia opposite Kenneth Branagh's Hamlet. What's more, *Sense and Sensibility* had picked her up an Oscar nomination. More than just talented, she was determined. She telephoned James Cameron to *demand* the role in *Titanic*. She explained her general philosophy on casting: 'The worst thing that can happen is that someone is going to think I'm a complete idiot and I don't really care. I just want them to know that I really want this job, I can really do this job.

'I called James Cameron on his mobile – I think he was in his car on the Los Angeles freeway – and I said, "You don't understand, I *have* to do this film. You cannot *possibly* cast anyone else in this role"

'He told me that the film would be brutally hard and maybe even dangerous. I didn't care. I just shouted: "Let's go for it!"'

Not a very British way perhaps, but it worked. Cameron was more than impressed.

As the initially stand-offish Philadelphia beauty she has to swim with the masses. ' I was plunged into freezing water and I was glad I had trained hard for the swimming sequences.'

Cameron had encouraged her to work with a trainer as the demure actress explained: 'I'd never done that before but I knew how important strength would be in the film. I only lifted light weights, about five pounds. I had to keep the length in the muscle because back then those sort of women didn't have any muscles. They never lifted anything. They even had to have someone to help them get dressed.'

She says she admired DiCaprio's guts, especially when he was nearly crushed to death by a horse during filming. 'He slipped and fell under the horse but he went on with the filming, on with the show.'

Winslett also suffered. She had a chipped elbow bone and gashed her knee. 'I looked like a battered wife', she says. 'Some days I'd wake up and think: "Please God, don't let me die."'

Before the movie was released she was keeping quiet about the conclusion. And about almost everything involving her 'close friendship' with Leonardo DiCaprio. Except for one 'little anecdote'. She says that during filming DiCaprio would look at her and ask:

'No, really, do you think I'm good-looking?'

Some days I'd wake up and think: 'Please God, don't let me die.'

POSTSCRIPT

FAME NOIR

"FAME IS NOT THE WORST THING. I WENT TO DINNER THE OTHER NIGHT AND THE GIRLS IN THE RESTAURANT IGNORED ME. IT WAS SO ANNOYING"
LEONARDO DiCAPRIO
1997

By the start of 1998, Leonardo DiCaprio was rapidly becoming a major name in both art house and blockbuster movies.

Titanic was afloat and following that there was the whirlwind costume adventure of *The Man in the Iron Mask* and the then untitled Woody Allen movie.

But just as eagerly awaited was the outcome of another project, a film version of *The Talented Mr Ripley*, the landmark novel of the late Patricia Highsmith. The Texas-born author had exiled herself to Europe living in England, France and, finally until her death in 1995, in Switzerland on the $6,800 Alfred Hitchcock had paid her for the film rights to her book *Strangers on a Train*.

Her fans – and the critics – believe her award-winning initial Ripley adventure to be her finest work. It was turned into a film by prominent French director Rene Clement in 1959 under the title *Plein Soleil*. It made a star of Alain Delon, who played Highsmith's pet psychopath Ripley, often with his shirt off and showing his taut tummy, his 'six-pack' of muscle.

In early 1998, nearly forty years later, the plan was for DiCaprio to take off his shirt and take on the role of the handsome, amoral Ripley. Further heightening the excite-ment was the involvement of British director Anthony Minghella, 'hot' from the runaway success of his adaptation of another book, *The English Patient*.

The film seemed right for DiCaprio. He had literally got his feet wet in *Titanic* and won his spurs with *The Man In the Iron Mask*. Here was a chance to enter the world of classic film noir, perhaps even to emulate one of his screen heroes, Robert Mitchum.

To DiCaprio, Mitchum was a man with integrity who had been able to work the studio system to his benefit, going through the motions in some movies, but also appearing in some classics. It was the sort of career worth aiming for.

DiCaprio liked the fact that after a family funeral Mitchum's ashes were cast across the rolling surf of the Pacific, that the actor elevated the cliché 'tough guy' to new heights of dignity by playing the part so well. Privately, Mitchum wrote and read poetry and always had about him a thoughtfulness that rarely interfered with his work as the big, commanding Hollywood package, who seemed to have been born to wear a trenchcoat.

Raymond Chandler advised authors who were having problems with plot to have a man walk through the door

☆ From blockbuster to film noir. Leo contemplates the future.

☆ Whilst filming his dual roles in *Man in the Iron Mask* Leo went to the Louvre to see the *Mona Lisa*. He was chased from the museum by screaming girls who tried to tear the shirt from his back.

with a gun. In the movies, Mitchum fulfilled that purpose. And, especially in the beginning, he played by the rules, at least those dictated by film noir. Important among them was: action isn't character, attitude is.

No studio ever made more melodramas than RKO, which was the B-movie factory of the 1940s. Mitchum once wryly commented: 'I used to wear the same raincoat. They just changed the leading lady.' The apotheosis of the genre, of the Mitchum character, was

Out of the Past, released in cinemas worldwide fifty years ago:

'I don' t want to die,' Jane Greer cries into Mitchum's hooded eyes.

'Neither do I, baby,' Mitchum replies, 'but if I do, I want to die last.'

Much of Mitchum's work relied on timing. Ironically, when he died obituarists noted the enduring power and renewed popularity of the type of films he helped establish, as another generation of film-makers and stars like DiCaprio were revitalizing them. Hence, half a century on cinema entered a new period of *new* noir.

It began at the start of the decade with British director Stephen Frears' *The Grifters* and James Foley's

☆ Spot the headband! Leo's hidden grooming secret is he's worn a tiny wire headband to hold back his forelock since he was eighteen.

After Dark, My Sweet. The source materials were works by author Jim Thompson, the cult icon of *Pulp Fiction*. Following on from the success of Quentin Tarantino's *Pulp Fiction* were *L.A. Confidential*, based on the 1990 novel by James Ellroy and *This World, Then the Fireworks* developed from a Jim Thompson short story. Kim Basinger was the star of 1950s-set *L.A. Confidential* – as a mysterious Hollywood good-time-girl in the *femme fatale* tradition of Lana Turner and Jane Russell – and she and the film were greeted by rapture at the 1997 Cannes Film Festival.

This is in part Mitchum's legacy, which he has left to young stars like DiCaprio. Mitchum never regarded himself as achieving the status of a cultural metaphor through movies he could film in a week, but for all his ironic detachment – 'I'm just a starlet' – he was elemental in a deep way.

Hopefully, Leonardo DiCaprio has many years to get somewhere close. But there is the grand American tradition of fast-lane living and tragic endings, a history from Billy the Kid to Elvis to Kurt Cobain and River Phoenix.

It is a tradition of flaws being cultivated as cool.

DiCaprio admits: 'My own life could have gone a different way, rebelling against the whole thing and going off the rails completely.

'But I think it's more important to adapt to your own life and escape from that. I've seen drugs, I've seen kids doing it, grown up seeing it, ever since I can remember. I don't know if it was instinctive or not but I never wanted to be part of *that*.

'I don't want to be thought of as a party animal. You know, the stereotypical young actor. I'm not like that. I don't enjoy what drugs do. I don't do anything but drink every once in a while.

'Shit, I'm happy the way I am. I don't

want to complicate stuff. I'm not Superboy. The only difference in my life is I have to be nice to people now. Before, if I didn't want to talk to someone I'd just say "Fuck off!" But I don't go to extremes. I'm not a normal human being ...

'I don't have emotions about a lot of

I rarely get angry, I rarely cry. I don't get sad and I don't get enormously happy.

things. I rarely get angry, I rarely cry. I don't get sad and I don't get enormously happy. I think a lot of people who talk about all that kind of crap are lying. I'm just trying to maintain happiness and that's all I really care about.

'Anyway at my age there's not much besides sex that's on your mind. Certainly not drugs – or that scene. I thought it was just a scummy sort of thing. My father who knows all about it, and is a 1960s person, really taught me a lot of things about the destruction of it.

'I'm just getting going. I told you before – I'm just starting to fly.'

'Don't wait up for me to crash.'

Television:

TV Commercials: *US Government, Disney Company and various others (1988)*

TV acting debut: *Lassie (1989)*

TV primetime début: *The Outsiders (1990)*

TV regular role: *Parenthood (1990)*

TV series: *Growing Pains (1991–1992)*

Films:

Film début: *Critters III (1991)*

First leading role: *This Boy's Life (1993).*
    With Robert De Niro and Ellen Barkin.

What's Eating Gilbert Grape? (1993)
    With Johnny Depp and Juliet Lewis

The Quick and the Dead (1995)
    With Sharon Stone, Gene Hackman and
    Russell Crowe

The Basketball Diaries (1995)
    With Mark Wahlberg

Total Eclipse (1996)
    With David Thewlis

Romeo and Juliet (1996-97)
    With Claire Danes and John Leguizamo

Titanic (1997-98)
    With Kate Winslett

The Man in the Iron Mask (1998)
    With Jeremy Irons, Gabriel Byrne, Gerard Depardieu,
    John Malkovich, Anne Parillaud and Judith Godreche

Picture credits:

Sylvia Norris, Hollywood

Hollywood Superstore Collection

Worldwide Syndication

Douglas Thompson Movie Stills Archive

Sources other than author interviews:

New York Times

Ocean Drive Magazine

Movieline Magazine

Details Magazine

Premier Magazine